Sincerely –
John W. Winkley

JOHN MUIR, *Naturalist*

Muir family on porch of Muir Manor

Muir Glacier

John Muir

Muir Home, taken about 1925

JOHN MUIR, *Naturalist*

A Concise Biography of the Great Naturalist

BY JOHN W. WINKLEY, M.A., D.D.

Published by the John Muir Historical Park Association, Martinez, California.

This book is published on behalf of the movement to purchase and restore the John Muir Home in Martinez, California, and the historic Martinez Adobe near it, to be maintained as part of a Muir Memorial Park.

—THE TRUSTEES

Printed by
THE PARTHENON PRESS
Nashville, Tennessee

JOHN MUIR, Naturalist

Copyrighted 1959

BY JOHN W. WINKLEY

CONTENTS

FOREWORD

John Muir, Scotch-born, Wisconsin-bred, made Yosemite and then Alhambra Valley his home for the rest of his life. It took this foreign born prophet to recognize that unless something was done before it was too late, much of the glory of the natural scene of the West would be mutilated and destroyed.

He led the way and through his inspired writings influenced others to aid him in his work for preservation, so that now much of his "pure wildness" is reasonably safe.

It is most fitting that the home of this great man in Alhambra Valley should be restored and preserved to honor him. It will serve as a shrine to attract and inspire his disciples to continue his brave and effective battle for conservation.

WILLIAM E. COLBY
Big Sur, California.

CHAPTER ONE

BOYHOOD IN DUNBAR, SCOTLAND

On the bleak north coast of Scotland near the Firth of Forth stands the little city of Dunbar. The massive ruins of the ancient Dunbar Castle, more than a thousand years old, lie on one of its jutting headlands. The waters of the stormy North Sea surge to and fro along the rocky shores. Here in Dunbar was the childhood home of the great naturalist, John Muir.

The ancestry of John Muir, especially on his father's side, is obscure. The first Muir known to the records was a John Muir, grandfather of the naturalist. He was a soldier in the British Army and married an English girl, Sarah Higgs, in London. They had two children, Mary, born in 1793, and Daniel, born in 1804. The parents died soon after Daniel's birth and a relative took the children into his home on a farm at the village of Crawfordjohn in Lanarkshire, Scotland. Crawfordjohn was about thirty-five miles southeast of Glasgow in a country of mountains and moors. Nearby flowed Duneaton River, a dashing, songful tributary of the Clyde. John Muir, the naturalist, once wrote: "Some of my grandfathers must have been born on a muirland, for there is heather in me, and tinctures of bog juices, that send me to Cassiope, and oozing through all my veins, impel me unhaltingly through endless glacier meadows, seemingly the deeper and danker the better."

Crawfordjohn probably had been the childhood home of grandfather Muir. Here at least Daniel Muir, the naturalist's father, "lived the life of a farm servant, growing up a remarkably bright, handsome boy, delighting in athletic games and eager to excel in everything. He was notably fond of music, had a fine voice, and usually took a leading part in the merry song-singing gatherings of the neighborhood. Having no money to buy a violin when he was anxious to learn to play that instrument, he made one with his own hands, and ran ten miles to a neighboring village through mud and rain after dark to get strings for it." So wrote John Muir in a brief obituary notice at his father's death.

Daniel's sister, Mary, married Hamilton Blakeley, a farmer at Crawfordjohn, and she took Daniel into her new home—practically "became a mother to him." John Muir's sketch of his father's life, continued, "While yet more boy than man, he suddenly left home to seek his fortune with only a few shillings in his pocket, but with his head full of romantic schemes for the benefit of his sister and all the world besides. Going to Glasgow and drifting about the great city, friendless and unknown, he was induced to enter the British Army but remained in it only a few years, when he purchased his discharge before he had been engaged in any active service. On leaving the army he married and began business as a merchant in Dunbar, Scotland. Here he remained and prospered for twenty years, establishing an excellent reputation for fair dealing and enterprise. Here, too, his eight children were born, excepting the youngest who was born in Wisconsin."

John Muir wrote of his father's character: "His life was singularly clean and pure. He never had a single vice excepting the vices of over-industry and over-giving. Good Scripture measure, heaped up, shaken together, and running over,

10

he meted out to all. He loved little children, and beneath a stern face, rigid with principle, he carried a warm and tender heart. He seemed to care not at all what people would think of him. That never was taken into consideration, when work was being planned. The Bible was his guide and companion and almost the only book he ever cared to read."

John Muir's mother, Ann Muir, was a Gilderoy, a name famous in Scottish border lore. Frequently it was spelled Gilroy or Gilrye. Her grandfather, James Gilderoy, had two sons, John and David, the latter becoming the "grandfather Gilrye" of John Muir's book, "The Story of my Boyhood and Youth." David Gilrye at twenty-seven years of age settled in Dunbar in December, 1794. Six months later he married Margaret Hay of the numerous and famous Scotch clan of that name. They became the parents of a large family of children, three sons and seven daughters. But they suffered a tragic loss of the three sons and five of the daughters who died in childhood or youth. Only Margaret the eldest and Ann the youngest survived to old age.

Daniel Muir met and married a woman of means in Dunbar who enabled him to purchase his release from the army, as John noted in the obituary, and to set up as a merchant. They had one child, but mother and child passed away after a brief period. Some years later Daniel met Ann Gilrye, the daughter of David Gilrye of Dunbar, and married her on November 28, 1833. They made their home in a large house directly across the street from father Gilrye's place, a happy circumstance for the Muir children. To Daniel and Ann Muir were born seven children here, and one later in Wisconsin. These were Margaret, Sarah, John,

David, Daniel, Mary, and Anna. Joanna arrived in Wisconsin. John's birthday was April 21, 1838.

Of Ann Gilrye Muir, John's mother, he once wrote: "She was a representative Scotch woman, quiet, conservative, of pious, affectionate character, fond of painting and poetry." Reared in a strict Covenanter tradition she was loyal to her religious teachings, yet tolerant of her son's scientific studies and conclusions. To John in California she wrote: "Your enjoyment of the beauties of California are shared by me, as I take much pleasure in reading your accounts." Daniel, however, was of a different mind. Being a strict Bible literalist, he condemned his son's nature pursuits as sinful and contrary to the Word of God.

John Muir as a boy under three years of age learned his letters from his "grandfather Gilrye," who as he led his little grandson along the city streets pointed out the letters on the signboards. At his third birthday he was enrolled in the village elementary school under Mungo Siddons, a stern and thorough master. A few years later his teacher in Grammar school was Master Lyon. Both exercised "an uncompromising tyranny" over their charges. Failure to commit a lesson to memory was cause for a thrashing both at school and later at home. Of this schooling Muir later wrote: "Old-fashioned Scotch teachers spent no time in seeking short roads to knowledge, or in trying any of the new-fangled psychological methods so much in vogue today. There was nothing said about making the seats easy or the lessons easy. We were simply driven point blank against our books like soldiers against the enemy, and sternly ordered, 'Up and at 'em. Commit your lessons to memory.' If we failed in any part however slight, we were whipped;

for the grand, simple, all-sufficient Scotch discovery had been made that there was a close connection between the skin and the memory, and that irritating the skin excited the memory to any required degree."

These were harsh measures but John Muir profited by them. During his school days he committed to memory the entire English, French, and Latin grammar books, and also three fourths of the Old Testament and ALL of the New Testament. One might reasonably suppose that such compulsory learning would leave in the heart of a child a legacy of bitterness and resentment. But John Muir loved his New Testament and always carried one with him on all his travels.

One of the schoolhouses of Dunbar stood by the sea-wall, and in great storms waves would splash over the wall upon the playground. Muir greatly enjoyed this manifestation of sea power, and took many walks along the shores with "grandfather Gilrye," who called attention to the crabs, eels and other strange creatures in the tide pools. This long familiarity with the sea caused Muir to record in his book "A Thousand Mile Walk to the Gulf," a nostalgic recollection from his childhood. "Today I reached the sea. While I was yet many miles back in the palmy woods, I caught the scent of the salt sea breeze which, although I had so many years lived far from sea breezes, suddenly conjured up Dunbar, its rocky coast, winds and waves; and my whole childhood, that seemed to have utterly vanished, in the new world, was now restored amid the Florida woods by that one breath of the sea. Forgotten were the palms and magnolias and the thousand flowers that inclosed me. I could see only dulse and tangle, long winged gulls, the Bass Rock

13

in the Firth of Forth, and the old castle, schools, churches, and long country rambles in search of birds' nests."

Near the close of his life Muir published his book, "The Story of my Boyhood and Youth." He devoted fifty pages to reminiscences of his childhood days at Dunbar. He recalled with feeling his intimacy with "Grandfather Gilrye." Each evening he crossed the street to the Gilrye home where he recited his lessons to him. David Gilrye was a lover of gardens, flowers, seashore, mountains, lakes, streams, and every wild thing. John instinctively followed the gleam. On a ramble with his grandfather in haying time he recalled that they sat down on a haycock in a large field. John's sensitive ear caught a faint squeak of pain from some tiny creature below. His grandfather thought it was only the wind. But John dug deeply into the hay and found "a mother field mouse and half a dozen young hanging to her teats. This to me was a wonderful discovery. No hunter could have been more excited on discovering a bear and her cubs in a wilderness den."

In his third reader at school were two favorite stories that helped to guide his interest and mold his character. One was entitled "Llewellyn's Dog" whose name was Gelert. Boy and dog wandered away on a long ramble into the wilds, alarming the family. At length the dog, covered with blood, returned home without his little master. The father, thinking that the dog had slain his boy, killed him. But a great hunting party finally found the boy,—"happy and smiling among the grasses and bushes beside the dead, mangled wolf" where the faithful dog had left him to bring help. Muir said that he and his classmates read the story over

14

and over, weeping bitterly over the fate of the innocent and loyal creature.

The other story was found in Southey's poem of "The Inchcape Bell." The good priest, the Abbot of Aberbrothok, had placed a bell on a dangerous rock at sea. Storm waves would cause the bell to ring, giving sailors warning of their peril. Ralph the Rover, a pirate, planned a joke on the good Abbot by cutting the rope and sinking the bell. Then he sailed away on long voyages of plunder. Long afterward he was returning to Scotland on a dark and stormy night, his shameful deed forgotten. He listened for the Inchcape bell in vain. Then as his ship struck the rock and began to sink, he recalled his wickedness, and "cursed himself in his despair."

One of the myths that plagued the children of Dunbar was the story of the "Dandy Doctors." These men, the servant girls said, wore long, black cloaks; carried rolls of sticking-plaster; and prowling the streets at night, caught unwary children. They covered their mouths with the plaster so they could not scream, then choked them to death. The bodies they sold to medical schools for dissection. In the early darkness of one winter day as the children were leaving for home, someone screamed that he had seen a "Dandy Doctor." The children huddled in the school-building, refusing to leave until Master Siddons escorted them up Davel Brae Hill and well on their way home.

The Muirs were lovers of flowers and cultivated a beautiful garden of them. John, mindful of the rules, left them strictly alone, though he loved them dearly. Down town, however, was the lovely garden of Peter Lawson, druggist and physician. John often snatched a blossom from Peter's

15

garden and slipped away. One day Peter caught him in the act. He dragged him to his stable where he kept his riding pony, a wild creature which usually reared up and jumped about when his master mounted him. All the children feared the fierce creature. Peter opened the stable door and pushed John in behind the pony's feet and closed the door. John, in mortal fear, remained absolutely quiet until released. It was a lesson he never forgot.

On Saturday nights the Muir children were given their baths by the servant girls. John was sitting on a stool, waiting his turn. Sarah, an older sister, wishing the stool, simply pushed him off, causing him to strike his chin on the edge of the tub. His tongue, which happened to be between his teeth, was badly cut. The doctor put a wad of cotton, soaked in an astringent, under his tongue and told him to keep his mouth shut. But as he dropped off to sleep that night he swallowed the wad and imagined that he had swallowed his tongue with it. His screams brought his mother in haste, but she only laughed at his fears. In after years his sisters often teased him when he talked too much, saying that it was a pity he hadn't swallowed at least half of his long tongue.

One of the favorite playgrounds of Dunbar children was the massive ruins of Dunbar Castle. It was over a thousand years old and had been the scene of numerous savage battles. The boys climbed over its lofty, crumbling walls and pinnacles regardless of danger to life and limb. Muir, in after years, on a visit to the Castle ruins, marveled at the skill and risk of these childhood feats which a well-trained mountain-climber would not attempt. The buried bones which the children found in the Castle grounds they dreamed were those of ancient warriors.

The Muir children knew many ghost stories, and one room upstairs in the Muir home was steeped in dark traditions. The house had formerly belonged to a physician and this room still held much medical apparatus: test-tubes, retorts, flasks, etc., once used by the dead doctor. John and David had the room next to this haunted one, and often at night dared each other to enter its ghostly interior. The one who went the farthest into the room and stayed the longest was the hero of the evening.

Another escapade of the boys was to climb out of the dormer window onto the slate roof and hang to the sill while the wind ballooned their nightgowns. Then they would hang on by one hand, and next by one finger. John achieved another daring stunt. He crawled onto the steep slate roof, around the window, and up to the roof top. He managed to get back safely, and David performed the same dangerous feat. But astride the roof top his courage failed him and he began to cry that he could not get down. John climbed out of the window and caught David by a heel as he slid down the roof, and slowly worked him around to the window and safety. The boys realized their folly and went shivering to bed.

Fist fights were a common practice among the Dunbar boys. These were not generally angry encounters, but tests of skill and endurance. The best fighter won a greater glory than that of becoming the top scholar. They also fought pitched group battles with snowballs or chunks of sand and sod, shouting their battle cries. Another contest was between two boys each with a selected bundle of green switches. Holding left hands they thrashed each other until one cried "quits" or sank in exhaustion. That game must have crossed

17

the ocean, for it was a contest of the writer's childhood in southern Indiana.

John Muir, pointing out the natural savagery of boys, admitted that they took delight in tormenting dogs and cats. They chased one old tomcat, stoned and badly bruised him. Another was caught and carried to the top of a house and dropped to the ground to test the old saying that a cat had nine lives. Then they pitied him as with swollen back and bruised chin he limped away.

John Muir and other Dunbar children loved to ramble into the open country on Saturdays when the weather permitted. Most parents, including the Muirs, forbade the children to leave their own yards. Disobedience was followed by a severe thrashing. Yet, regularly as Saturday came around, John and David slipped away on country excursions, stoically taking the punishment. They were fond of birds, especially the skylark, which would spring from the ground and soar heavenward, singing as it climbed into the sky. Though lost to sight, its song could still be heard. Once they found a nest of young skylarks and took one home with them. They nourished it with care and it rewarded them with sweet singing. But it would often gaze at the sky with apparent homesickness which gave the boys a guilty feeling. Eventually they took it back to its native field and opening the cage let it dart into the heavens. It was quickly out of sight but its song of rejoicing thrilled and repaid them.

Shipwrecks were frequent along the rocky Dunbar coast and once a vessel loaded with apples went aground. The boys had a merry time, diving into the waters and snatching the fruit as it bobbed along on the waves. Other times more precious cargoes broke upon the shores and the whole population rushed to salvage what they could from the wreckage.

It is interesting and may be useful to know what food sustained these active children of old Dunbar. Breakfast consisted of oatmeal porridge with milk; dinner (at noon) was a meal of broth, boiled mutton and a barley scone; there was an after-school tea, of a slice of white bread, butter and a barley scone; and supper in the evening of a boiled potato and another barley scone. This was not much variety, yet it was evidently wholesome and sufficient.

In John Muir's grammar-school reader (Maccoulough's Course of Reading) there were some natural history stories that made a deep impression upon him and prepared him for a sudden change in his life. One was a story told by the Scotch ornithologist, Wilson, who had traveled widely in American forests. This contained incidents in the life of a bald eagle and a fish hawk. The habit of the hawk was to circle over a stream or pond, plunge into the water on seeing a fish, and catching him, fly away for a feast. But the eagle, watching him from a nearby perch, would swoop upon him, forcing the hawk to drop his fish. Quickly the eagle would dart under the falling fish, catch it and fly away to his nest.

Another story in the book was by Audubon who described flocks of passenger pigeons which numbered millions of birds darkening the sky over vast areas of country in America in their flight. In roosting in forest trees at night their weight frequently broke off large limbs. Farmers would attack them at night, killing them with clubs, and heaping them in huge piles for their hogs to eat. And in

19

these same American forests were wonderful trees which gave a sap that boiled down to delicious syrup or sugar. Into the minds of the children filled with these wonderful stories came the news of fabulous amounts of gold discovered in that land beyond the sea.

Thus in the spring of 1849 came a startling announcement to the Muir household. John describes the incident in these words: "One night when David and I were at grandfather's fireside solemnly learning our lessons as usual, my father came in with news, the most wonderful, the most glorious, that wild boys ever heard. "Bairns," he said, "you needna learn your lessons the nicht, for we're gan to America the morn!" They were amazed, bewildered, yet overjoyed. As John related it,—they had dreams of "trees full of sugar, growing on ground full of gold; hawks, eagles, pigeons, filling the sky; millions of birds' nests, and no gamekeepers to stop us in all the wild, happy land."

Grandfather Gilrye gave each of the boys, John and David, a gold coin, but looked very sad, realizing that his old age would be made lonely by the departure of his grandchildren. His parting words to them that evening were: "Ah, poor laddies, poor laddies, you'll find something else over the sea forbye gold and sugar, birds' nests and freedom fra lessons and schools. You'll find plenty hard, hard work."

To his schoolmates on the street that evening John heralded the news: "I'm gan to America the morn." To their expressed doubts of this, he exclaimed—"Weel, just see if I am at skule the morn."

CHAPTER TWO

YOUTH ON A WISCONSIN FARM

The decision of Daniel Muir to emigrate to America with his family was evidently a very sudden one. Apparently it came as a total surprise to everyone. There was no intimation that he had any such plan, though the idea must have been growing in his mind. To the children, especially to the older boys, John and David, it held promise of a glorious adventure. The father decided to take only part of the children with him at once—Sarah, the second daughter, John and David. The mother with Margaret and the three younger children—Daniel, Mary and Anna would follow when a house had been built for the family in the new land. John was now eleven years of age.

That next morning Daniel and the three children took a train to Glasgow. There they boarded a vessel sailing for the new world. They were going, as John expressed it, to "the wonderful, school-less, book-less, American wilderness." The speed of sailing vessels was slow, and this one took six weeks and three days to make the crossing. To John and David everything about the ship and sea was full of interest. They were on deck every day regardless of weather, watching the sailors at work and listening to their songs. The captain often invited the boys into his cabin and gave them books to read. He seemed surprised at their perfect English accent, and their knowledge of French and Latin. But the experience of the father, Daniel, and sister Sarah, was very different. They had to go to their rooms in rough weather, and suffer the "miseries of sea sickness."

There were many emigrants to America on board the vessel and much discussion among them regarding the best region in which to settle. It had been Daniel's intention to go to the woods of upper Canada. But most of the other emigrants insisted that the forests of Canada were too dense and difficult to clear for cultivation. They argued that Michigan or Wisconsin offered better opportunities. In addition a grain dealer at Buffalo told Daniel that most of his wheat came from Wisconsin. This piece of news settled the matter for him. He had his goods sent westward to Milwaukee where he found a farmer with a wagon who offered to haul his goods to the village of Kingston about a hundred miles to the northwest. This was on the border of the vast, unsettled wilderness. The man charged thirty dollars for the haul, a price which he soon regretted. The road was muddy and Daniel's load heavy with machinery, furniture, kitchen utensils, and provisions.

However they arrived safely at Kingston, where the children were boarded with a family until Daniel could locate a quarter-section of land in an unclaimed area, and build a temporary shelter. Then he had three yoke of oxen, hitched to a big wagon, haul his goods and children to the new home. The little shanty stood in a sunny, open space in the forest overlooking a little lake and a flowery meadow. Here the children were immediately at home in this fresh and glorious wilderness. John said that they were "utterly happy" among the wild birds, frogs, snakes, turtles, trees, and flowers. On their arrival, John and David immediately found a blue jay's nest in a tall tree and climbed up to it to view the beautiful green eggs. The handsome birds noisily objected to their presence. On the following day the boys climbed again to the nest but to their surprise found it empty. The parent birds had carried their eggs away. How they did it was a mystery. Did they carry the eggs in their bills? And what did they do with them while they built a new nest? John said he never could solve that mystery, and never knew any ornithologist who knew the answer either.

All about this living wilderness were innumerable other birds of every size and color—brown thrushes, bluebirds, song sparrows, kingbirds, hen hawks, whippoorwills, woodpeckers, etc. One of the most interesting of them was the kingbird, which, though small compared with many birds, was master of all. When marauding hawks and jays came near his nest he angrily chased them out of the neighborhood. Once, Muir said, he was greatly amused to watch the kingbird drive away a big, clumsy hen hawk, darting at him and striking him on the back of his head. Finally, wearied with that, he alighted on the hawk's shoulders, and scolding and pecking at him, rode him away like a boy riding an obstreperous wild horse.

As soon as settled in the little shanty, Daniel hired a Yankee to help him clear some of the land for cultivation. John got a good share of piling up and burning the logs and brush. It was hard, tiresome, work but he toiled manfully on without complaint. The boys plied the Yankee with questions. One evening a strange bird came near their cabin door and startled them with his cry, "Whippoorwill." "What's that?" they asked in wonder. The Yankee replied: "He is telling you his name and he wants you to whip poor Will." Here was another marvel of this strange new land. Likewise the night hawk surprised them. This bird lays its eggs on the bare ground, and when discovered, limps away as with a broken leg or wing. When the intruder follows the apparently injured bird, to a safe distance from its nest, it suddenly flies away, returning by a roundabout way to its eggs or young.

Another new experience came to the children on one sultry evening as they sat by the shanty overlooking the lake and the flowery meadow. The air over the meadow became filled with thousands of little flashing lights which glowed for a moment, then vanished. John could not believe his eyes, and asked David whether he saw this unusual spectacle. David replied yes, and so they sought an explanation from the Yankee. "Just lightning bugs," he said, and led them down to the meadow where he caught some of them in a little glass. At the house the boys watched them in fascination, as their lights glowed and faded away.

Through all that spring and summer this region was a bird paradise. There was the partridge drumming his "Boomp, Boomp, Boomp" like a woodland ghost. And there the boys heard the lovesong of the jacksnipe as on swift wing-beats it wheeled, darted, and looped over the meadow. Most of the birds migrated to warmer lands in the autumn. Only a few remained through the severe winters—the nuthatches, chickadees, owls, prairie chicken, and quail. Sometimes a few stragglers of ducks, hawks and jays remained behind. With the first touch of spring came the bluebird with its welcome song, followed by the robins who bravely built their nests in the gardens of the settlers in a confident fellowship with their human friends. Soon a host of sweet singers—thrushes, bobolinks, red-winged blackbirds, meadowlarks and the song sparrows, would appear. The Baltimore oriole would build its hanging nest, and the scarlet tanager flash its gay costume in the sunny forest openings.

But some of the scenes and sounds of Muir's day have long since vanished. No longer do the prairie chickens with their little families stroll trustingly around the farmyards. Gone are the wild ducks, and the beautiful wood ducks from the swamps, ponds and streams. And the graceful swans and the Canadian gray goose are seldom seen in flights overhead. The passenger pigeon has ceased to exist. Man's thoughtless, heartless destruction of these wild creatures has made the world poorer.

John Muir had an amusing experience with that strange bird, the loon. He wrote that it had "a strange, sad, mournful, unearthly cry, half laughing, half wailing." They were so wary that few hunters ever bagged one. Muir found one on Fountain Lake one winter day and stunned him with a bullet. He carried him home and put him on the floor by the kitchen stove. There he sat, quiet and motionless, with head erect and small, black eyes watchful. The house cat, old Tom, awakening from sleep, gazed in astonishment at the strange bird, then fled wildly to the farthest corner of the room. Observing the silent creature for some time, he cautiously approached him. The loon slowly, imperceptibly, drew back his long neck, head, and pick-like bill in a double curve and waited. The cat, creeping slowly forward, came within reach of that long neck, when, with lightning speed, the loon struck. With a resounding whack the cat was hit between the eyes. He bounded into the air with a screaming, explosive "Wuck," and rushed madly around the room trying to escape. Finally he settled down in a far corner, rubbing his wound and glaring at his foe with low growls.

The wilderness farm held many other interesting creatures. From the swamps came the songs of the hylas with the bullfrogs joining the chorus, booming their "Drunk, Drunk, Drunk; jug-o-rum, jug-o-rum." Soon after the family had arrived at the farm a neighbor gave the children a little dog, which possessed surprising intelligence and endurance. He could whip any dog in the surrounding country and had a keen sense of smell. One evening as the family was at prayers the dog, Watch, was lapping up his milk from a large pan. Through an open door zoomed an enormous beetle, which after a few flights around the room, dived into the pan of milk. Watch jumped back in alarm, then walked around the pan, sniffing, growling and barking at the splashing bug. Fearing their father's wrath, the children restrained their mirth though almost choking with the effort.

Snapping turtles were common on the farm. The boys encouraged Watch to tease one, but it caught an ear of the dog, and held on. Watch, holding his head to one side, ran about, howling with terror and pain, to the great amusement of the boys. But John admitted that this was shameful fun. Eventually Watch acquired a bad habit of catching and eating little chicks, at home and at neighbors'. For this he had to be put away to the deep sorrow of the children.

For the farm work Daniel purchased several yoke of

oxen and the boys soon discovered that they possessed individuality like themselves. When tired their eyes showed a human likeness in feeling and when hungry, an appealing look. When given food and allowed to rest there was an expression of gratitude. They had a love of play and an attachment for one another. A white-faced ox, named Buck, was unusually intelligent. The other oxen could not eat pumpkins unless these were split in pieces with an axe. But old Buck would go to a pile of them, select a good one, push it into the open and kneeling down with his head upon it, crush it with his weight. Then he arose and ate it at his leisure.

The oxen could follow a trail in darkness by their sense of smell. Once Daniel was driving a yoke of them home at night, drawing a load of provisions. They suddenly stopped and refused to go any further in that direction. Daniel unhitched them, and holding onto the tail of one of the oxen was led safely home. The next morning he found the wagon at the edge of an impassable swamp. On dark, rainy nights they would find their way home, following the trail by scent like dogs.

When the Muirs left Scotland, Daniel promised the boys a pony. He now kept his promise and brought home from Kingston a handsome Indian horse. A Winnebago had raised him and taught him to carry loads, stand without being tied, walk or run as desired, and fear nothing. Daniel taught the boys to ride him. John mounted him first. His father said, "Whup him up, make him gallop." The pony dashed away and when John cried "Whoa," he stopped so quickly that John went flying over his head. Remounting, he rode swiftly back. Another "Whoa" sent him

27

hurtling into his father's arms. This happened several times, then David rode the pony with similar results.

But they soon mastered the art of riding and could guide the pony without rope or bridle by leaning to one side or the other as Indians do. On the farm were sunken places called "kettles" caused by glacial action. Some of these were eighty feet long and twenty feet deep, sloping down and up at the ends. The boys learned to ride the pony at full speed into and out of these kettles without going over his head into the kettle or off his tail on the way out. Jack, the pony would do anything the boys asked him to do— swim a pond, jump a ditch, climb a bank. Once John made him jump toward the opposite bank of a twelve foot wide stream. Jack couldn't make it and landed in deep mud. Unable to extricate the pony, John ran for help. His father, with ropes and a yoke of oxen, hurried back with him. Only the pony's head was then above water. They quickly got a rope around his neck and pulled him to safety, unharmed except that he was plastered with mud.

In the autumn the new house was finished and Mrs. Muir, Margaret and the three younger children, Daniel, Mary and Anne, arrived from Scotland. Now all were together again, and family life went on smoothly except for those frequent whippings which Daniel gave to any disobedient or careless child. On one occasion John tied his father's whip to the dog's tail and he ran away into the woods losing the whip. The father called John in for a thrashing, and sent David out to cut a switch. David finally returned with an oak limb ten feet long and two inches thick at the butt. Daniel stormed at him hotly, not seeing any humor in the situation. He had waited so long that now he was called away on an errand and John escaped his punishment for once.

An errand which John or David had to do each day was to bring in the cows with the pony in the evening. If they failed to show up on time, the pony would go alone and bring them in, biting them on the rump if they failed to obey. After a few years Daniel bought two work horses for the farm work, Nob and Nell. Then he sold the pony to a man who was going to California. This was a cruel thing to do, for the loss of the intelligent, faithful animal caused the boys deep anguish. Immediately the care of the two horses fell to John. He discovered a strange difference in the disposition of the two mares. Nob was intelligent and affectionate, while Nell was sulky and obstinate. Once an Indian stole Nob and tried to sell her in a distant town. But someone saw that she had worn shoes and harness and seized her. An advertisement in a paper brought about her recovery. John wrote of Nob, "She was a great pet and favorite with the whole family. She quickly learned playful tricks, came running when called, and seemed to know everything we said to her. She had the utmost confidence in our friendly intentions."

But Nob met a sad and untimely end. She was overdriven by Daniel on a hot, sultry day to Portage and back, twenty-four miles. Her lungs became inflamed and she passed through two weeks of terrible suffering. She would come to one of the family and lay her head on his or her lap with an appealing look in her eyes. All the family stood about her weeping as she passed away. John said of her: "She was the most faithful, intelligent, playful, affectionate, human-like horse I ever knew, and she won all hearts."

29

Fountain Lake and its surrounding meadow were a constant source of interest and pleasure to John. In the shallow water grew the pure white water lily and on shore the wild flowers and lady slippers. The meadow bloomed in autumn with asters, goldenrod, sunflowers and daisies. On the borders were strawberries, dewberries, cranberries and huckleberries. In the woods were hickory nuts, hazel nuts and wild apples. The boys learned to swim in the lake like frogs, but once John came near drowning. On a Fourth of July the boys and some friends were boating, swimming and fishing there in deep water. John, confident of his skill in the water, attempted to swim from shore out to the boat, but his hand slipped as he reached for it, and his movement pushed him under it. He became frightened and sank to the bottom. He came up again but confused, sank once more. Then, remembering that he could swim under water, he made his way to a shallow spot and cried for help. The boys came quickly to his rescue.

This was a humiliating incident, and that night John went back to the lake alone, to recover his confidence. He rowed out to the deepest part, dived to the bottom, and came directly up again. This he did over and over again, saying as he dived, "Take that," implying his mastery both of himself and the water. He never again feared the deep water and became an excellent swimmer.

Unending toil filled the lives of the early settlers. They were up before dawn and toiled until after dark. They harvested wheat, corn, potatoes, until the fertility of the soil was exhausted. Then they planted clover to restore it. Patches of ground planted to watermelons and muskmelons produced enormous crops to the delight of all.

Springtime work was enjoyable, but the summers were exhausting. In winter there was stock to feed, tools to grind, wood to cut, fence rails to make. They were busy as ever, shelling corn, fanning wheat, making axe handles, and other odd jobs.

In spite of the fact that they felled forests and burned vast piles of logs, the only fire in the Muir home was in the kitchen stove. They dressed in freezing cold rooms, forcing their frost-bitten feet into stiff boots or shoes. But there were compensations. The skies on winter nights were calm and clear, sharp and brilliant with stars. The Northern Lights were magnificent. As the snow storms raged, they remarked, "Jennie is plucking her doos" (doves). At times sleet storms would turn the forests in sunlight into a world of flashing diamonds.

The first settlers in this wilderness had no roads, only Indian trails and animal tracks. There was little news of the outside world. The nearest neighbor of the Muirs was four miles away. Yet in a few years all of the land was occupied by newcomers. A schoolhouse was built which was used also as a church. Daniel Muir was a religious fanatic in beliefs though sincere and devoted in spirit. Anything not contained in the Bible was of questionable value, and anything in addition to its teachings was surplus. The family was held to long sermons, long dreary services, long prayers. Daniel moved from one denomination to another as some notion might strike him. Upright, just and kind in intentions, he was a victim of limited education and misguided zeal.

During eleven years on this farm, John Muir did the work of a full grown man, digging out stumps, ploughing root-filled ground, planting and cultivating crops. Even when sick he was held to his tasks. He was the rail-splitter, 100 a day. He kept ahead of the hired men, the champion wheat-cradler, binding, stacking, thrashing the grain. He helped to keep the farm and buildings neat, clean and beautiful with flowers. After the Fountain-Lake farm was well under cultivation, Daniel bought another quarter section of land four miles away, which became the Hickory Hill Farm. Thus the back-breaking toil of clearing a place from forest jungle began all over again. And there was another problem, no nearby stream or source of drinking water. A well had to be dug down through sandstone, ninety feet deep. Every bit of the work fell to John, as Daniel was no hand for such work. Let down in a bucket John toiled till noon, then again to nightfall, until the job was done. It was a beautiful rounded well when finished.

But John had his diversions, the pleasures of a keen, alert, observing mind. Honey bees were imported from Europe, and reached Wisconsin about ten years later. John saw them at work among the flowers and discovered an easy method of locating a hive. He took a little box of honey to an open place on a hill and sat down. Soon a honey bee buzzed along and accepted some of John's honey. On leaving for the hive, he made observations of the area, John, a stump, some trees. Then got his bearings and made a "bee-line" for home. Soon he was back for more honey. John noted the direction of his flight and then changed his location. The bee found him on another hill top, took more honey, and went home. Muir calculated the two lines of flight to a junction and found the hive there in a hollow log.

CHAPTER THREE

A WILDERNESS EDUCATION

John Muir's boyhood in that beautiful Wisconsin wilderness was filled with nature education. He went on to more formal education. At an early date a schoolhouse was built in the neighborhood, but John spent only a few months in school there. For the most part his Dunbar schooling was beyond anything offered here. When about fifteen years of age John began to hunger for more knowledge and persuaded his father to buy an advanced arithmetic. His father approved his ambition so long as it did not interfere with the farm work. In his spare moments that summer John thoroughly mastered the arithmetic, then went on to algebra, geometry, and trigonometry, and reviewed grammar.

His father had only a few religious books, but some of the neighbors had other reading mattter, among them the novels of Scott. Daniel disapproved of such writings, but John devoured them secretly. Then he persuaded his father to buy copies of Josephus' "War of the Jews," and d'Aubigné's "History of the Reformation." Plutarch's "Lives" was forbidden as the work of an old pagan, until the graham bread and antiflesh craze reached the neighborhood. Daniel thought these might have some information on the foods of the ancient Greeks and Romans that made them strong and healthy.

On the food craze Daniel accepted the antiflesh theory

and became a vegetarian. But Mother Muir insisted on putting both meat and vegetables on the table, permitting each to make a choice. John came to the help of his mother, by citing the story of Elijah and the ravens. He pointed out that the Lord fed Elijah not on bread or vegetables alone but on flesh also. Daniel immediately was convinced and admitted his error.

While money was scarce, John did manage to earn and save a few pennies which he invested in Shakespeare, Milton, Cowper, White, Campbell, and Akenside. But he could snatch only a few minutes a day for reading. After evening prayers all were immediately ordered to bed. If John read briefly by a light in his room and the father observed it, he was compelled to stop. Finally Daniel said to him that if he must read, he could get up as early in the mornings as he chose. Daniel never supposed that a weary boy would awake from sound sleep. Here was John's great opportunity. He arose at one o'clock thrilled with five hours of free time for reading or work on his inventions.

Since reading in an unheated room in winter was too unattractive, John went to the basement to whittle, saw, and build his inventions. He made his own tools, a fine tooth saw of a strip of steel from an old corset. He made bradawls, punches, and a compass. At hand were a vise, files, a chisel and a hammer. The cellar was directly under his father's bedroom and the noise disturbed him, but he had given his word and would not interfere.

Soon John had a large array of inventions finished—a self-setting sawmill which he put into operation at a nearby stream, water wheels, door-locks and latches, thermometers, pyrometers, clocks, a barometer, a lamp-lighter, a

34

fire-lighter, a machine for early or late rising, and an automatic device for feeding horses. Most of the machines he figured out for himself, having never seen anything like them. A masterpiece was a clock that would tell not only the minute and hour, but day of the week and of the month. It would operate a bedstead, setting the sleeper on his feet at any given time. It would start fires, light lamps, etc. The father disapproved of such nonsense (as he considered it), but did not interfere. When his masterpiece was finished, Margaret observed her father secretly get down on his knees and examine the intricate machine, apparently proud of his son's ability to make such things, yet he offered no encouragement.

Next John invented a clock in the shape of a scythe to represent Father Time. A bunch of arrows for a pendulum indicated the flight of time. Underneath were the words, "All flesh is grass." This clock pleased his father and all the family admired it. After fifty years it was still keeping good time. John started to build another clock with four large dials, one for each of four directions. This he wanted to put on the barn or a large tree, but this his father would not permit, saying that the neighbors would trample down his garden and fields in looking at it. A thermometer which he invented was so sensitive to heat that the warmth of a man's body five feet away would make the hand on the dial move quickly. Neighbors and the family, including Daniel, regarded this as a marvelous creation. People urged him to exhibit his inventions at the State Fair in Madison.

John Muir once wrote that his mother had expressed a hope that he would become a minister. His sisters, he said, wanted him to become a great inventor. His own dream in youth was to be a physician. But he saw no way by which he could get the necessary education. Then a friendly neighbor suggested if he would follow his advice and exhibit his inventions at the State Fair, he would quickly find many machine-shop owners who would offer him good wages for his work. Thus he could earn sufficient funds for his education. John was convinced and made preparation to go to the Fair at Madison. On leaving home he asked his father whether he would help him, if at any time he should be in desperate need of some money. Daniel replied, "No, depend entirely on yourself." That sounded more harsh than he meant for at later times he did send him some money. John's cash on hand was $10.00 which he had earned by sale of some produce from a patch of ground which he had cultivated, and the gold coin which his grandfather Gilrye had given him on leaving Scotland.

David drove John to Pardeeville, nine miles away, where he might take a train to Madison. He had never been there before. He had with him two clocks and a thermometer, roped together but unwrapped. At the tavern where he spent the night the tavern keeper asked about John's strange machines. At Muir's reply, he inquired where he got his patterns. John said, "In my head." Soon a crowd gathered, and the tavern keeper explained the machines, while John kept in the background, noting their interest and admiration. At the train in the morning the conductor advised him to give his bundle to the baggage master, fearing a crowd might collect around John on the train. John asked the engineer to permit him to ride on the engine so that he might study its working. The engineer consented, provided John would come into the cab at the stations so the Company would not criticize him for breaking a rule. John greatly enjoyed the ride, the first train he had been on since leaving Scotland.

In Madison, inquiring his way to the Fair Grounds, he shouldered his bundle and at the gate applied for permission to exhibit his machines. The gate keeper took one look at the contrivances and excitedly exclaimed, "Oh, you don't need a ticket, come right in." He sent John to the Fine Arts Hall, where a dignified gentleman greeted him and asked what he had to exhibit. On beholding the clocks and thermometer, he exclaimed with surprise, "Did you make these?" He continued to admire them, saying that he was sure that they would attract more attention than anyhing else in the hall. He then called a carpenter and directed him to make shelves and anything else that John might need for his exhibit. The clocks and thermometer did attract wide and enthusiastic attention and the Fair Board gave him a prize of $15.00 and a diploma. Later Muir learned that the dignified gentleman who had greeted him in the Hall of Fine Arts was at that time professor of English Literature at the University of Wisconsin.

John was offered a job by the owner of a machine shop in Prairie du Chien, which he accepted. He soon found, however, that the man was frequently away from home and there was little work for him to do. He then found a family, named Pelton, for whom he could work for his board while studying mechanical drawing, geometry and physics. After some weeks John decided to return to Madison and make an effort to get an education. There he earned a few dollars making and selling some of his bedsteads that set people on their feet at a given time in the morning. He also earned some money addressing circulars in an insurance office, and paid his board by taking care of a pair of horses. His persistent ambition now was to enter the State University.

One day while roaming around the University grounds, admiring the lawns, flowers, trees and buildings, a student who had seen John's exhibit at the Fair, recognized him and stopped to greet him. John said, "You are a fortunate fellow to be allowed to study in this beautiful place. I wish I could join you." The youth replied, "Why don't you?" Muir said that he didn't have enough money, to which the boy rejoined that little money was required; that one could board himself, live on bread and milk for a $1.00 a week. This little talk gave John new courage and hope. He went to the Acting-President, Dr. Stirling, and explained his case, his schooling in Scotland, and his efforts to study and read good books at odd moments snatched from long, laborious days on the Wisconsin farm.

Dr. Stirling had a warm place in his heart for such youth, ambitious for an education that seemed beyond their grasp. He welcomed John to the University, had him assigned a room in the dormitory and placed in a special preparatory class. The dormitory janitor told him to come to the furnace room and cook his meals, which consisted of bread and molasses, graham mush, and baked potatoes. John's effective schooling in youth and self-taught courses on the farm—English, French, Latin, literature and science subjects—now quickly came back to mind, and in a few weeks he was dismissed from the preparatory class and admitted to Freshman standing.

Once again John's inventive genius served him well. One day he was exhibiting his mechanical bedstead operated by a clock. Two boys, one a son of Prof. Ezra Slocum Carr, teacher of Natural Sciences at the University, and the other a son of Dr. James Davie Butler, Professor of Greek, were acting as occupants of the bed. To the surprise and keen enjoyment of the crowd, at a given moment on the clock, the mechanism of the bed set the boys on their feet on the footboard. The friendship of the boys with Muir soon brought him invitations to the homes of Drs. Carr and Butler, where he became a frequent and appreciated guest. Both families became life-long friends of Muir, especially the wife of Dr. Carr, Jeanne C. Carr, a native of Vermont, a very gifted woman and a devoted botanist.

John Muir had returned to Madison in the closing days of 1860 and now at twenty-two years of age was pursuing his favorite studies at the University. His keen, alert mind and friendly spirit made him a marked man among the students and with the faculty. To save time and facilitate study he invented a mechanical desk that popped up a textbook for an allotted time, then another and another. His strange, handmade inventions, set up in his room, brought a horde of visitors, students, faculty and strangers, to see them. Many thought it was a section of the College museum. Not all of his contraptions were utilitarian in purpose. He had also a "loafer's chair." This chair had a seat with a cunningly devised crossbar which under a certain squirm of a sitter's body fired off a pistol. This never failed to send the unsuspicious victim into a wild leap, to the vast amusement of all.

John, not knowing how long he would be able to stay in

39

College, did not follow the prescribed courses of study, but selected those which he thought would be of most value to him in life. His room-mate during the second year was Charles E. Vroman, who described their room as lined with John's shelves, one above another, on which were stored retorts, glass jars, tubes, botanical and geological specimens, and numerous mechanical contrivances. Of John Muir he wrote: "When telling me stories of his early life, or reading Burns, he often dropped into a rich Scotch brogue, although he wrote and spoke English perfectly. The only books which I remember seeing him read were his Bible, the poems of Robert Burns, and his College text-books . . . he was the most cheerful, happy-hearted man I ever knew."

The summer vacation periods John spent on the Muir farms, working in the harvests. The summer of 1861 he was with his sister Sarah and her husband, David M. Galloway, who then owned the Fountain Lake farm. John cradled four acres of wheat a day, and helped shock it. Then the evenings he spent in his botany studies. The summer of 1862 he worked on his father's place, the Hickory Hill farm, doing similar work. Thus he earned much of his college expenses, though he admitted that at times he had to cut his food supplies to fifty cents a week.

Toward the middle of the second school year, he decided to teach a country school at Oak Hall ten miles south of Madison. The salary was $20.00 a month, with "boarding around at the homes of patrons." He managed to keep up his University courses by studying at night. During the first few days of teaching under the critical eyes of his pupils he felt shy and awkward, but soon he had won all hearts. The winter mornings were very cold and it was the teacher's chore to start the schoolhouse fire and have the room warm before the children arrived. This took much of John's scarce time. So he rigged up an ingenious contraption that would start the fire for him at the proper time. He explained the process: "I had only to place a teaspoonful of powdered chlorate of potash and sugar on the stove hearth near a few shavings and kindling, and at the required time make the clock, through a simple arrangement, touch the inflammable mixture with a drop of sulphuric acid."

His farmer host doubted his ability to perform this feat. So John, on leaving the school building one night, arranged kindling and wood in the stove with the mixture on the hearth. He set the clock to drop the acid promptly at 8 A.M. That next morning he invited his patron to watch from their window with him, and sharply on time a column of smoke arose from the schoolhouse chimney. Through that entire winter John's mechanism never failed to start the fire for him.

In the spring term John was back at the University again pursuing his studies. On one June day he was standing on the steps of North Dormitory, when a fellow student, named Griswold, stopped by his side. Griswold plucked a bunch of blossoms from an overhanging locust tree and asked Muir to what family it belonged. Muir said he did not know, never having studied botany. Griswold said it belonged to the pea family, which John thought was ridiculous, noting the vast difference in size. Griswold replied that size had nothing to do with it. He then displayed the similarity of petals and shape of stamens and pistil, of

41

seeds, and leaves, etc. and that there was a similar taste in locust and pea leaves. This was a first lesson in botany for John Muir, and it opened a vast new world of exploration to him, one he followed enthusiastically all the rest of his life. Soon he was abroad into the country-side searching for plants, dissecting them and tracing their family connections and learning their names. In a letter to his sister, Sarah, he wrote: "You would like the study of Botany. It is the most exciting thing in the form of even amusement, much more of study, that I ever knew." And he added a little note of personal successes: ". . . I was elected judge in one of the debating clubs a short time ago, also President of the Young Men's Christian Association."

The years John Muir spent at the University of Wisconsin, 1860-63, were Civil War years, and his sensitive nature was deeply touched by the terrible carnage and suffering of the boys in the armies, and the grief that struck and over-shadowed their homes. One of the large training camps for the Union Armies was Camp Randall, located about a half mile from the University Campus. John was a frequent visitor there, endeavoring to counsel and comfort these lonely, homesick boys. While there is little record of his work with them (he apparently never referred to it in his books or letters), yet there are fragments of his correspondence with many of these lads in the service which show his tender interest and religious counsel like that of an un-official chaplain. Perhaps the frightful unsanitary conditions of the army camps during these war years had much to do with John's dream and hope of becoming a physician, a purpose which was clearly in his mind at the close of his University career.

In early June of 1863 Muir wrote to his sister Sarah and her husband David Galloway, that he with two friends were going on a geological and botanical trip down the Wisconsin River into Iowa. The story of this tour was told in some letters which he wrote to his friend, Miss Emily Pelton of Prairie du Chien, letters which he composed and predated some months later and mailed to her as giving the freshness of being written "during the Ramble." The first letter was predated July 7th, 1863, at McGregor, Iowa. This town was across the Mississippi River from the junction of that stream and the Wisconsin. He described the delightful scenery along the Wisconsin River as it plunged along its way through deep, narrow canyon walls below beetling bluffs overhead. Someone had told them of a romantic glen filled with ancient fossils with an old log house at its narrow entrance. In late afternoon from the high canyon walls they spied the log house far below and struggled down to it. To their amazement they found an almost deserted, ruinous house, with four gaudily dressed women sitting in a row opposite two old men, in a desolate, unfenced yard. They knew little about a romantic glen, could give no directions to it, and spoke in a strange, weird speech and tones. John wrote: "We then took alarm, gained the summit of the bluffs after an hour's hard labor, built our camp-fire, congratulated each other on our escape, and spoke much from the first chapter of Proverbs."

A second predated letter related the experiences of the boys boating on the Mississippi River and attempting to sail home up the rushing waters of the Wisconsin. First, however, after the visit to the strange company at the log house and their night on the high bluffs, they located the

43

"romantic glen" and found numerous fossils and many new specimens of flowers. Boating on the "Father of Waters" was delightful, but sailing or rowing up the Wisconsin was a different story. They could make no headway against the swift stream and stopped for a night, in which they made some long sturdy oars. But these were of no avail and, setting the boat adrift on the waters, they shouldered their packs and "soberly marched away" toward Madison. At evening time they reached a beautiful home, where after a most wearisome walk, they found an old lady who invited them in for a night's lodging and gave them a bountiful supper, the first real meal in several days. She said that she had a son who once on a long journey in New Mexico had been refused food and shelter at night during a storm. The story of his experience had made her determined, though sometimes imposed upon, she would deny hospitality to no one. After more toilsome, hungry travel, they arrived safely at Madison.

Another letter written to Sarah and David Galloway, undated, but probably composed in the last week of July, 1863, related the adventures of a brief trip to the famous "Wisconsin Dells" on the River above Portage. John and a friend took the train to Kilbourn Station above the Dells and on a raft which they made, floated down stream between the perpendicular, sandstone walls, which broke into fernery dells and side ravines of glorious beauty. Muir described them: "Those ravines are the most perfect, the most heavenly plant conservatories I ever saw. Thousands of happy flowers are there, but ferns and mosses are the favored ones. No human language will ever describe them." And of the last ravine down stream he wrote:

"The rocks overhang and bear a perfect selection of trees which hold themselves toward one another from side to side with inimitable grace, forming a flower-veil of indescribable beauty. . . The walls are fringed and painted most divinely with the bright green polypodium and asplenium and mosses and liverworts with gray lichens. . ."

Soon afterward Muir was back in Madison and took his departure from the University. Standing on a distant hilltop he bade a sorrowful farewell to the scenes of his college days. But he wrote: "I was only leaving one University for another, the Wisconsin University for the University of the Wilderness."

CHAPTER FOUR

BOTANIZING IN CANADA

In the closing days of his study at the University of Wisconsin, spring of 1863, John Muir's plan was to enter the medical school of the University of Michigan at Ann Arbor. Some letters from Madison friends addressed to him there were returned to them unclaimed. Among them was a letter of Prof. James R. Boise, giving an introduction and recommendation for Muir to the faculty at Ann Arbor. But Muir never reached the Medical School. The only explanation he ever gave was in a letter to a friend in which he wrote: "A draft was being made just when I should have been starting for Ann Arbor, which kept me at home."

That summer and autumn Muir worked in the harvest fields of Fountain Lake farm for his brother-in-law, David Galloway. It is probable that he was hoping to earn enough money to enter the Medical School at a later date. During his spare time on the farm he continued his botanical studies, sitting up to late hours analyzing strange plants. In February of 1864 Muir wrote to Emily Pelton that he would soon be leaving the Galloway home for a botanical trip, but insisted that he had not given up his dream of entering the Medical School at some future time. A month later he again wrote to Miss Pelton, saying: "I am to take the cars in about half an hour. I really do not know where I shall halt."

From later records it was learned that he went northward into Canada on a long botanizing tour. His exact course remains unknown. However, Dr. William Frederic Bade, editor of his journals, made a fortunate discovery of Muir's herbariums used on his travels in Canada. These he left at the Charles W. Moores home in Indianapolis. In them Muir had recorded the time and place of discovery of each plant. The locations were mainly in the Province of Ontario, between the Georgian Bay of Lake Huron and Lakes Ontario and Erie to the south.

Muir described the region as: "very uneven and somewhat sandy; many fields here are composed of abrupt gravel hillocks; the inhabitants are nearly all Irish." There were extensive tamarack and cedar swamps dotted with beaver meadows. In one of these vast swamps Muir spent most of a day struggling over logs, brush, and tangled vines, apparently endless. With the sun sinking low in the west and his strength well-nigh spent, he suddenly reached an open area and a house. He wrote: "I will not soon forget the kindness shown me by an Irish lady on emerging from this shadow of death near her dwelling."

On a later occasion Muir had a similar experience, this time in the Holland River swamps north of Toronto. He had been rambling all day through majestic forests and over meadows covered with a boundless profusion of wildflowers. Toward evening, caught in the great swamp, he feared he would have to build a nest in some tree in which to spend the night, free from water. Here he made a discovery of the rarest and most beautiful of the flowering plants "Calypso Borealis." It stood alone on a little mossy bank. He wrote: "It seemed the most spiritual of all the flower people I had ever met. I sat down beside it and fairly cried for joy." Somehow it seemed to soothe his hunger and weariness, and he soon reached a house on a hill. A Scotch woman received him kindly, saying: "Mony a puir body has been lost in that muckle, cauld, dreary, bog and never been found. It's a God's mercy ye ever got out."

When Muir left the University of Wisconsin he promised to write at least once a year to Prof. J. D. Butler. He now wrote to him describing this flower and his experience in the swamp. The story so impressed Prof. Butler that he sent the letter to the Boston Recorder which printed it. Muir said that this was the first of his writings to appear in print.

On Muir's rambles through Canada that summer he often ran out of money to buy food. Then he would ask for work chopping wood, clearing a piece of land or harvesting grain. He slept wherever night overtook him. Once in a maple grove he was awakened by howling wolves nearby. As he arose to replenish the fire a large wolf dashed by within a few feet of him. He slept no more that night, but kept his fire burning brightly.

Most of the families in this latter area were Scotch, and to his great pleasure one day he found a family who had lived in Dunbar. They had a happy time together talking of people and incidents of their childhood home. Here also he found a Scotch Highland family by the name of Campbell, a mother, daughter, and two grown sons. They took him into their home like a long lost relative. With them he stayed a month working on the farm and in off hours wandering through the Holland River swamps. The mischievous boys played many jokes on him. One morning he had arisen early and gone botanizing in the forest. Mrs. Campbell called him to breakfast several times. Going

49

to his bedroom she saw the covers pulled over his head. She called again and still receiving no reply, she turned the covers back, only to find a sack of rags in his place. "Oh" she exclaimed, "those boys, those boys."

Deserters from the British Army sometimes hid in these swamps, and at that very time officers were searching for one of them. The boys told the officers that a strange man had been seen in the forest nearby, and they captured him. Muir said he had a difficult time convincing them that he was not a deserter but only a botanist..

This Scotch community was composed of pious and loyal church people, but in spite of their toilsome, impoverished lives they had many joyous social times together. This was especially true of the young people who had their "singing schools," social games, and a particularly good time at "sugaring off." This gathering was in the springtime when the maple sap was running and the farmers were boiling it down to syrup or sugar. Couples could stretch the stiff syrup into long ropes between them with many changing stunts. And the "wax" made delicious eating. They seldom indulged in dancing as their pious elders disapproved of it.

John and his younger brother Daniel were both away from the Wisconsin home and through letters discovered that they were in this same region. Daniel had obtained employment at a sawmill in Trout Hollow near the town of Meaford on the Georgian Bay. Here he had been working for about six weeks when John found him. They arranged to take a botanical trip together for several weeks, then returned to Trout Hollow where both obtained work at the mill for the winter. This mill manufactured rake and broom handles. John invented a machine that would more than double the output. Mr. William Trout, the owner, readily agreed to the change and made a contract with John for a thousand dozen rakes and thirty thousand broom handles.

John Muir in a playful letter to his sister Mary described the inmates of the Trout home where he and Daniel boarded as "our family." William Trout, the head of the house, was "an unmarried boy of thirty summers who is going to elect a lady mistress of Trout's Hollow some day." There were two sisters of Mr. Trout, Mary and Harriet, one was the housekeeper and the other a schoolteacher. With them lived Trout's partner, Charles Jay, "a bird of twenty-five." John remarked: "We all live happily together."

Through the winter of 1864-65 the mill was a busy place and John as usual drove himself on a busy schedule of work and study. He built one of his clock-bedsteads that would set him on his feet at five o'clock each morning. Some mornings when he happened to be sleeping diagonally across the bed he was thrown to the floor with a loud bump. This awoke all in the house and aroused a peal of laughter.

As spring came, Daniel wanted to return home, but John stayed on for another year. In a letter to Emily Felton, he exulted in the glories of his "romantic hollow." "Freshness and beauty are everywhere; flowers are born every hour . . . our world is indeed a beautiful one, and I was thinking on going to church last Sabbath, that I would hardly accept a free ticket to the moon or to Venus, or to any other world; for fear it might not be so good." In December of 1865 John wrote to his sisters, Mary, Anna

51

and Joanna, saying that he was exceedingly busy, trying "to do at least two days work every day, sometimes three. I sometimes almost forget where I am, what I am doing, or what my name is." But he insisted that it kept him from getting homesick. He mentioned a letter from Daniel who said he had "plenty of money, clothes, and hope for the future."

One Sunday as Muir was sitting in the house alone, reading a book, a little bird flew into the house and was caught by the cat. Muir chased and caught the cat and tried to make him release the bird. As the cat held onto his prey Muir tightened his grip on the cat's neck until he unintentionally choked him to death. When the family came home, they teased him by saying: "John is always scolding us about killing spiders and flies, but when we are away he chokes the cat." They would go around the house slyly saying, "Poor Kitty."

During this winter he kept up a delightful correspondence with the Carrs of Madison. Mrs. Carr's letters were a source of inspiration and joy to him. He told her that he wished he could go back to college, could get away from machines, could study medicine and do something in lessening human misery. But how, and when? He assured her, "O how frequently, Mrs. Carr, when lonely and wearied, have I wished that like some hungry worm I could creep into that delightful kernel of your house— your library."

Muir's inventive genius continued to be manifested in other machines to make rake teeth, handles, bows, with greater speed. By March, 1866 the thirty thousand broom handles were finished and stored in the factory for seasoning. Then on one stormy night the building burned to the ground with all its contents. The owners had no insurance, and this made them bankrupt. John accepted a note of indebtedness to be paid at some future date. To the credit of Trout and Jay every cent of this indebtedness was paid.

John now felt that there was nothing left at Trout Hollow for him to do, and it was time for him to seek other adventures. He gave many of his books to the boys of his Sunday school class and some botany books to interested friends. He left behind a large circle of folk to whom he had endeared himself. They wrote to him may times in after years saying that their circle would always be incomplete without him and they wished those happy days might return. But that "Trout family" was soon scattered far and wide over Canada.

John decided to go to Indianapolis, Capital of the State of Indiana. In one of his reminiscences he said: "Looking over the map I saw that Indianapolis was an important railroad center and probably had manufactories of different sorts in which I could find employment, with the advantage of being in the heart of one of the very richest forests of deciduous hardwood trees on the continent." There he soon found employment in a carriage factory at $10.00 a week; second week, $18.00 and soon this was advanced to $25.00 a week. His inventive genius again came into effect and he produced and installed better machinery. Though absorbed in this interesting work, he did not forget his beloved trees and flowers. One of his letters at this time reported: "When I first entered the woods and stood among the beautiful flowers and trees of God's own garden, so pure and chaste and lovely, I could not help shedding tears of joy." The owners of the factory wanted John to accept a foremanship in the factory and eventually become a partner in the business. But John could not agree to this, since the winsome voice of nature was calling him again to her wilderness paths.

The change, however, came sooner than he had expected. One day while installing a new circular saw, a piece of steel struck one of his eyes, piercing the cornea. In a few minutes the sight of the eye failed, and that night the other eye became blind also. Muir felt that darkness had closed on God's beautiful world forever for him. Prof. Butler who had learned that John was in Indianapolis sent him the address of some of his friends in the city. This family heard of John's accident and at once brought a noted oculist to see him. This doctor assured him, after examination, that the aqueous humor would probably be restored and that he would be able to see again about as good as ever.

Muir spent a month or two in a darkened room, but his loneliness was dispelled by friends who visited him, and as soon as light could be admitted to the room, read to him. Children brought him armsful of his favorite flowers.

Blessed with such friends, the dark days passed quickly away and John was able to resume his nature studies. About the middle of June 1867, he left Indianapolis, taking with him a young friend, Merrill Moores. He wanted to examine the flowers of the Illinois prairies at this time of the year. They went directly to Decatur in the center of the State and began working their way northward to Rockford and Janesville. They botanized for a week on the prairie seven miles south of Pecatonica. Then they started for Wisconsin, soon arriving at John's old home at Fountain Lake.

Many years later in an address to the Sierra Club in San Francisco John described Fountain Lake with its pond lilies, its carex meadows, and the nooks full of ferns and heatherworts, saying: "When I was about to wander away on my long rambles, I was sorry to leave that precious meadow unprotected; therefore I said to my brother-in-law: 'Sell me the forty acres of lake meadow, and keep it fenced, and never allow cattle or hogs to break into it, and I will pay you whatever you ask.'" But Galloway considered his plan wholly impractical. Muir urged him at least to preserve for him a small flowery, ferny bog, which he promised to do. However he later found the glacier bog trampled to ruin.

On the twelfth of August he wrote to a friend, Catherine Merrill, saying that he was bidding good-by to his folk on the old farm and to all of his old friends before leaving on a long journey, "for, I know not where."

CHAPTER FIVE

A THOUSAND MILE WALK TO THE GULF

After a week of botanizing with his friends, the Carrs and Butlers at Madison, John Muir left Wisconsin, outward bound to wander over all the earth. Wisconsin was never to be his home again. He went directly to Indianapolis to visit his friends there. Then he left by train for Louisville, Kentucky. A trip of exploration had been forming in his mind for many months. He proposed to walk southeasterly across Kentucky, Tennessee, a corner of North Carolina, and Georgia, striking the Atlantic Coast at Savannah. There he could take a ship to a port on the Florida Coast and walk across that State to Cedar Keyes on the Gulf. From that port he hoped he might find a ship which would take him to South America.

Muir left Indianapolis on the first day of September, 1867, and spent the night at Jeffersonville on the Ohio River. Crossing the River the next morning to Louisville, he passed through the city without stopping, steering his way by compass. A few miles out of town he stopped under a wayside tree, got out his maps and outlined his course to the Gulf. He proposed to avoid cities and towns and to travel by "the leafiest, wildest, and least trodden way I could find." He carried with him only a plant press, a small rubber bag which held a change of underclothing, a comb, towel, brush and three small books—a New Testament, Milton's Paradise Lost, and Burns's Poems. The first day he walked twenty miles, and at night "found shelter in a rickety tavern."

His course had been over river bottoms where "great oaks seemed to spread their arms in welcome." These Kentucky oaks he thought were the most beautiful he had ever seen. On the following morning glad to escape the dirty tavern, he took a road that led him into rolling hills, known as the Kentucky Knobs. Along the way he found the streams and wells salty. Reaching at noon a rushing stream he prepared to ford it, but a negro woman on the further shore warned him that he might be drowned and advised him to wait until she could send a boy with a horse. Soon a little negro lad, riding a white horse with "long, stilt legs" appeared, and with much "rocking and tumbling" got Muir safely across.

In the afternoon he came to a "genuine old Kentucky home," standing among orchards, corn fields and some wooded hills. The large, airy house, built in southern style, had a long central hall, which Muir said looked like a railway tunnel. Around the house was what appeared to be a village of farm buildings and negro quarters. Fruit was abundant everywhere. Toward evening, wearied with his travel, he simply lay down in some tall grasses and went to sleep. At early dawn birds awoke him with their chirping and scolding. By his side and bending over him were some strange, beautiful plants. He felt that this was a most delightful campground.

Once more on his way he walked ten miles to a region of black oaks known as the Barrens. On the road he frequently stopped to chat with farmers, "stout, happy fellows, fond of guns and horses." That night he reached a village which "seemed to be drawing its last breath." A friendly Negro guided him to a tavern. This was another squalid place from which he was glad to escape. This day, September 5th, he came into a region of caves. From the mouths of them cool breezes were blowing and ferns belonging to a northern clime clustered. By one cave he found a deep pool of cold water completely surrounded by shrubs, ferns, flowers, mosses, in such beautiful array that he lingered long in loving contemplation. At noon he arrived in Mumfordsville, and had a long talk with its headman and pioneer, Mr. Mumford. This man of broad culture and scientific learning, gave him much information on botany. In the afternoon his way led along a railroad where unkempt dwellings repelled him, and he spent the night in a schoolhouse among stately oaks, and slept on the "softest looking of the benches."

Next day, September 6th, Muir reached Horse Cave, and ten miles further the great Mammoth Cave. The region here was wild and beautiful. He did not linger long, apparently not entering the vast underground chambers. That night a school trustee entertained him and invited Muir to teach the winter term of their school. But Muir had other plans. He traveled the next day with a friendly Kentuckian who greeted all of the Negro men and women as "Uncles" and "Aunts." September 8th was a Sunday and Muir met many happy, smiling Negroes, dressed in their best clothes. They were on their way to church. The road now lay along the Cumberland River, a "happy stream" in which he took huge delight. Finding no family willing to receive him, he spent the night in the open, sleeping on a hillside.

September 9th, he crossed the State line into Tennessee, remarking that "Kentucky was the greenest, leafiest, State I have yet seen." The next day he was climbing the Cumberland Mountains, and in six hours had reached the summit which afforded a sublime view. While on this road he was overtaken by a youth on horseback who offered to carry his bag. Muir said it was no bother, but the boy insisted on taking it, rode briskly ahead, examining its contents, then brought it back to him. Evidently he thought it contained money. As houses were few in these mountains, he began to inquire for entertainment. But he warned the housewives that he had no change, only a five dollar bill. At last a blacksmith took him in without charge. He was a religious man and thought that Muir was wasting his time studying plants, until Muir recalled that Jesus said: "Consider the lilies, how they grow." That convinced him of his error.

Muir had a new adventure the next day. Ten mounted men barred his road waiting to rob defenseless travelers. He could not avoid them, so he marched straight ahead, greeted them smilingly, and passed on. They watched him with curiosity but let him go. Apparently they saw his plant press, and took him for a poor herb doctor without means. That night he got a meal from a Negro family but had to sleep in a field.

His walk on September 12th brought him to the Emory River. Of it he wrote: "Every tree, every flower, every ripple and eddy of this lovely stream seemed solemnly to feel the presence of the Creator. Lingered in this sanctuary a long time thanking God with all my heart for his goodness." He reached Kingston before dark and mailed his

60

pressed plants to his brother in Wisconsin. Then for two days he wandered over flinty ridges and winding valleys, once getting lost. He passed through a filthy village set in a beautiful surrounding and at the end of the second day reached neat Madisonville by the Unaka Mountains. A pleasant young farmer kept him overnight.

For some days he passed through a mountain area where small sums of gold could be mined, but the habitations were the most primitive in everything, which he had ever seen. On the 18th of September he crossed the North Carolina line into a beautiful forested country, causing him to exclaim: "Oh, these forest gardens of our Father, what perfection." He spent the night, however, with a man who was feuding with a neighbor, ready to shoot at sight.

Muir traveled along the leafy banks of the Hiwassee River, "its forest walls vine-draped and flowery as Eden." Then he was stopped by the sheriff at the town of Murphy for questioning, but released as harmless. In fact the sheriff invited Muir to stop with him for a day of rest in a comfortable home. Muir was soon across this narrow neck of North Carolina into Georgia. Here he had an amusing experience. For some miles over a hilly country he walked behind a wagon drawn by one very large mule and one very small one. In the ramshackle wagon rode an old woman, a young woman and a young man. Going up a hump in the road, all three would slide to the tail-gate with a slam. Then down the hump they skidded with a bang against the head board. All the while they kept up a merry conversation.

Now out of the mountains and along the Chattahoochee River, Muir found a Mr. Prater whom he had known in

Indiana. He was visiting relatives here. Prater took him boating on the River where the banks were overhung with muscadine grapes which the people there called "scuppernongs." The next few days his road led through brush and vines, among rattlesnakes and merry, easy-going Negroes. On meeting a white man, off would come their hats as smilingly they passed by. At length he reached the city of Athens, "a remarkably beautiful and aristocratic town containing many classic and magnificent mansions of wealthy planters." Muir said this was the only southern city, so far, that he would like to revisit.

Muir's journey now took him many miles across country to Augusta on the Savannah River. He had nothing to eat on the way, and in Augusta went hungry to bed. His funds were now almost exhausted. He got a cheap breakfast and followed down the river toward the coast. In a swamp land he saw his first Spanish moss festooning the trees. The wealthy planters seemed inhospitable, but one, a Mr. Cameron, became interested in his botanical collection and entertained him for a night. Mr. Cameron's hobby was electricity and he prophesied that it would eventually run trains, steamships, light houses and cities, in fact do the work of the world.

After more than a week of travel down the Savannah River through dank, dark swamp lands, Muir arrived in the city of Savannah by the sea. The money he expected from his brother had not reached there. He felt exhausted, lonesome and poor.

That first night in Savannah Muir spent in the cheapest lodging house he could find. In the morning he went again to the post office and express office, getting no word from home. Discouraged and weak from lack of food, he wandered out a smooth, white-shelled road which in three or four miles led to the beautiful Bonaventure Cemetery. The fields were ragged and desolate, the roadsides covered with rank weeds, and the ruinous log huts of the poverty-stricken inhabitants surrounded by broken fences. But the great Bonaventure Cemetery held a refreshing surprise for him. A hundred years ago it had been the country estate of a wealthy planter. Long, shady avenues of live oaks led to the great mansion, now in ruin. A little stream watered the place. Song birds were flitting about and singing everywhere. Said Muir, it was "so beautiful that almost any sensible person would choose to dwell here with the dead rather than with the lazy, disorderly living." Only a small part of the grounds was occupied with graves. The live oaks along the avenues were festooned with Spanish moss, which hung in long, silvery-gray skeins, eight to ten feet in length and, "slowly waving in the wind, produced a solemn, funereal effect. . ."

Muir returned to the city and sought a sleeping place among the flowery sand-dunes by the sea, his purse sufficient only to provide him with a loaf of bread. Idle, prowling Negroes were all about, and he feared for his life. Then he thought of Bonaventure Cemetery, just the place for a "penniless wanderer." The fear of ghosts would keep mischief makers away. Starting out the gleaming white road, he reached the graveyard at dark and lay down under a giant oak with a little mound for a pillow. In the morning he discovered that his bed was a grave, but he said he had slept about as well as the one below. Disappointed by the non-arrival of his express package, he built a little shelter of brush in a thicket of sparkleberry bushes in the cemetery and gathered long moss for a bed. Here, arriving after dark to avoid suspicion, he slept in peace, his meals a hunk of bread or a few crackers.

On the sixth day, to his great relief, the money package arrived. But the express clerk would not let him have it until he could be identified. Here was another difficulty, as no one in the city knew him. However, Muir's quick intelligence solved that problem. First he showed a letter from his brother in which he named the amount of money there was in the package, and when it was mailed. But the clerk said that wasn't enough, since he might have stolen the letter. Muir then pointed out that his brother referred to his botany work and specimens, saying that he might have stolen the letter, but he couldn't steal his knowledge of botany. "Examine me and see if I know anything about it," Muir insisted. The clerk laughed and called his boss, explaining the situation. The manager looked at the paper, then at Muir, and waving his hand, said: "Let him have it."

Muir pocketed the money and went out on the street where he met a Negro woman with a large pan of gingerbread. He bought some of it and marched happily along the street, munching the sweet, tasty bread as he went. Further along he stopped at a market and as he said, "got a large, regular meal on top of the gingerbread."

Now Muir entered upon another phase of his "Thousand Mile Walk to the Gulf." That same day on which the money arrived, he boarded a vessel, the "Sylvan Shore," for Fernandina, Florida. They sailed along the coast, part of the time out at sea and part of the time in the inland chan-

John Swett and John Muir

John Muir and John Burroughs

Dr. John Strentzel

Dr. John Strentzel looking from Muir House toward Martinez Adobe

Martinez Adobe

Helen and Wanda Muir, daughters of John Muir
Picture taken by William Keith, famous painter

Yosemite Falls, Yosemite Park

Mariposa, Big Trees in Yosemite Park

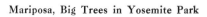

nels behind the reedy islands off the mainland. In a day and a half, the steamer reached the little, bedraggled port on the Florida coast, where the Captain discharged the passengers in the morning without any breakfast. Muir bought a loaf of bread and without asking a question of anybody, left the little town. He was now in the "Land of Flowers" and took the first road into the cypress groves and swamps. On a dry hillock he stopped to eat some of his bread. As he lay on his side, there came a rustling noise behind him. His weak, starved, lonesome condition made him a prey to his imagination. In fright his mind conjured up a large alligator with open jaws descending upon him. Instead he saw only "a tall, white crane, handsome as a minister from spirit land."

Muir's plan was to follow the railroad track across Florida to the Gulf at the port of Cedar Keyes. As he walked along the sandy track he beheld on either side strange flowers, vines, shrubs, and trees. Again and again he plunged into the coffee-colored water to secure specimens for his plant press. Then in a grassy, open place he caught sight of his first palmetto tree, to his unspeakable delight. The tree was about twenty-five feet tall, with fifteen or twenty leaves, each leaf ten feet in length, and there was an oval crown at the top. This was a day of wonders, strange plants, strange birds, strange winds, and strange sounds.

As evening came on he sought for a house and food, but none could he find. In the darkness he located a dry hillock, ate some bread, drank some of the brown water and went to sleep. In the morning, breakfastless, he continued on the flowery way until almost noon when he reached a logger's shanty where rough, barbaric looking men gave him some pork and hominy to eat. He was glad to go on his way. After a few days of such travel, sometimes in swamps, sometimes in sandy plains, he arrived at the attractive little town of Gainesville where he found food and lodging for a night. Muir had many unhappy experiences with the strange inhabitants of these regions until on the 20th of October he arrived at the home of a Captain Simmons, a wealthy, scholarly gentleman, who entertained him and invited him to stay for a few days. He suggested a hunting trip and a visit to the finest palmetto grove in the State. Muir doubted the wisdom of halting, but accepted the kind invitation. But in the visit to the swamp-surrounded palmetto grove, he lost his way and only by sheer luck recovered the trail to safety. He feasted that night on fresh venison, johnny cake, and sweet milk. Three days later, October 23rd, he reached the sea.

Muir described his approach to the Gulf in these charming words: "I was plodding along with my satchel and plants, leaning wearily forward, a little more sore from approaching fever, when suddenly I felt the salt air and before I had time to think, a whole flood of long dormant associations rolled in upon me. The Firth of Forth, the Bass Rock, Dunbar Castle, and the winds, and rocks and hills came upon the wings of that wind, and stood in as clear and sudden light as a landscape flashed upon the view by a blaze of lightning in a dark night."

Muir was now at Cedar Keyes on the Gulf of Mexico, where he hoped to find a ship sailing to South America. In the meantime he went to work in a lumber mill for a

Mr. Hodgson who took him into his large mansion home like a most welcome guest. But he was not well, and in a few days came down with a severe attack of malarial fever which kept him in bed or indoors for several months. Only the nursing skill, care, and unfailing kindness of the Hodgson family saved his life. While convalescing he enjoyed observing the ever changing sky, the colorful flocks of birds, and the flowery world about him.

One day in early January, 1868, a steamer, the Island Belle, stopped at Cedar Keyes, and Muir, bidding good-by to his gracious hosts, the Hodgsons, took passage to Cuba. There he hoped to find a ship bound for South America. On the Gulf a storm overtook the vessel and Muir surprised the Captain and sailors by remaining on deck enjoying the tumultuous and luminous waves surging about them. They soon reached the beautiful harbor of Havana, passing the massive, frowning Morro Castle at the entrance. The Captain invited Muir to make the ship his headquarters while in port as he expected to be there for about a month. Each day a sailor would row him ashore and call for him again in the evening.

The Island of Cuba was beautiful and he longed to explore it, but his feeble health would not permit him to go far afield. He did, however, go into the nearby surrounding country, observing the flowers, shrubs, trees and birds, and he gathered strange, beautiful shells along the shores. Havana had a large botanical garden where he spent many happy hours.

But Muir could find no ship going to South America. Instead he noticed in a New York newspaper an announcement of a ship leaving that port for California. He asked the Captain of the Island Belle about a passage to New York. The Captain pointed to a little schooner in the harbor which he said would leave for that city soon. He remarked: "You had better see the Captain at once for he must be about ready to sail." Muir made immediate arrangements with the Captain of the schooner to take him to New York, and going aboard, he left Havana early the next morning.

The little schooner was loaded with oranges, even the decks were piled high with them. They had a stormy passage. Flying fish would drop on the oranges where the ship's dog managed to catch and devour most of them. The trip required about ten days and they reached New York harbor about the middle of February. The steamer, Nebraska, would sail for Aspinwall in a few days so the Captain permitted John to sleep aboard his vessel in the meantime. New York City did not interest him. On February 22nd he went on board the Nebraska which sailed that day for the Isthmus.

CHAPTER SIX

ARRIVAL IN CALIFORNIA

The voyage across the Gulf of Mexico to the port of Aspinwall was interesting to Muir, but he said the crowd on board was a "barbarous mob, especially at meals." He had only half a day to ramble around the town. Then his train left for the Isthmus crossing along the Chagres River to the west coast. The glorious flowers and tropical jungles charmed him. In his diary he wrote: "I fairly cried for joy and hoped that sometime I should be able to return." Taking ship at Panama he arrived in San Francisco on March 27th.

With a laugh Muir often told of his arrival there. On the following morning, carrying his little bag and the plant press, he went out upon the street and asked the first man he met what was the nearest way out of town to the wild part of the State. The man, a carpenter, stared at him in astonishment, set his tools down, and asked: "Where do you want to go?" Muir replied, "Anywhere that's wild." The man directed him to the Oakland Ferry as a good way out of town.

Muir had become acquainted with an Englishman, named Chilwell, on ship-board from the Isthmus. He invited him to be his company on a walking trip to the Yosemite Valley, which Chilwell was glad to accept. Muir had secured a little pocket map of California and outlined a route of travel. They went up the Santa Clara Valley where the orchards, vineyards, and wheat fields were beautiful in springtime verdure. "The sky was cloudless and the whole valley was a lake of light." The ranges on either side of the valley were clothed with masses of wildflowers blending many shades of white, purple, and yellow.

Toward the head of the Valley they turned eastward into Pacheco Pass in the Coast Range, a region no less enchanting with flowers, the songs of quail and larks, and music of tumbling streams. From the top of the Range they caught a view of the widespreading San Joaquin Valley, one vast, level garden, "the floweriest part of the world I had yet seen," Muir wrote. Beyond were the lofty Sierra Mountains covered with snow. They hurriedly descended into the Valley which Muir estimated to be five hundred miles long and at least fifty miles wide. It was covered with wildflowers so dense that it seemed his foot rested on a hundred plants at each step.

Muir and Chilwell crossed the San Joaquin River at Hill's Ferry and followed the Merced River into the foothills around Snelling and Coulterville. An Italian storekeeper in the latter town sold them supplies for their mountain trip—flour, tea, salt, etc., and warned them that the mountains on the way to Yosemite were still covered with eight to ten feet of snow. He also urged them to take a gun along since there were dangerous bears in the region. Muir didn't think they would need one, but to please Chilwell they bought an old army musket with some powder and buckshot. Chilwell lamented their meatless diet, and hoped the gun would bring in some game.

In this, however, he was disappointed, since he was too poor a shot to bag quail, grouse, or hare, and Muir refused to shoot his little friends. They climbed rapidly up the snow-covered ridge to Crane Flat at an altitude of six thousand feet. Around them here was a magnificent coniferous forest and on the Flat a mountaineer's little cabin. Chilwell immediately appropriated it, since, as Muir said, he had the "house habit," but Muir made his bed on a cleared spot under a pine tree.

Muir had promised to teach Chilwell how to shoot, and now he gave him a first lesson. Chilwell pinned a square of paper on the house and went inside, shouting—"Fire away." After Muir fired, he came out screaming, "You've shot me, Scottie." He had leaned against the wall opposite the paper and some buckshot had gone through the half-inch boards. Asked why he did such a foolish thing he said: "I never imagined the _____ gun would shoot through the side of the 'ouse." But Chilwell had on three coats and three shirts for the cold weather, so was not badly hurt, though Muir had to pick out a few buckshot from his skin.

They advanced easily to the brow of the magnificent Valley, and caught a glimpse of Bridal Veil Falls which they estimated was about sixty feet high. Imagine their surprise when they reached its foot! Here the imposing walls rose hundreds of feet high in domes and pinnacles. For ten days they roamed this wonder-filled Valley, camping at the foot of Bridal Veil Falls one night, where a hungry bear disturbed them. They spent a sleepless night by a bright fire, sitting on guard with the gun.

Leaving the Valley by the south wall, they visited Galen Clark at his Wawona Station. After a pleasant night with Mr. Clark from whom they secured more supplies, they pushed on to the Mariposa Grove of big trees. Here they spent many days wandering from tree to tree, amazed at their colossal size and majestic stature.

As their supplies were now getting low and their funds gone, they decided to go down to Snelling and work in the wheat harvest. On the way down the ridge an owl lighted on a fence post near them. Muir suggested, since Chilwell liked meat, he shoot the owl for supper. Chilwell protested that a "howl" was not fit to eat, but shot him anyway and made soup of his body. He begged Muir not to tell anyone "as 'ow we 'ad a howl for supper." After the close of the wheat harvest, Chilwell departed on a course of his own.

Muir remained in the neighborhood breaking horses (mustangs) for a Mr. Egleston. Then he ran the ferry at Merced Falls and later made considerable money shearing sheep. In the neighborhood lived a queer character named John Connel, who went by the nickname of "Smoky Jack." He was an old bachelor who had grown wealthy raising sheep. Smoky Jack persuaded John that he would have no trouble herding one of his bands for which he needed a man at once. Muir decided to give it a try and took charge of a band of several thousand sheep quartered at a big corral in the nearby hills. He found there a little, dirty cabin, too filthy for use, so he made his bed outside. When he let the sheep out that next morning, they scattered in all directions, and he feared that he would never get them all together again. But at nightfall they came back to the corral of their own accord.

Winter rains began in December and grass, flowers, insects, birds, rabbits, all kinds of little creatures reappeared on hill and meadow. This region was known as "Twenty

Hill Hollow," which name Muir used as the title of a magazine article which he wrote some years later, describing this area. These autumn and winter jobs were only interim employment since Muir planned to return to the mountains in the spring. However he was troubled about sufficient funds to purchase food through the summer months.

At this propitious time Mr. Delaney, a neighbor of Smoky Jack, came to him with a proposition that seemed to fit his need. Mr. Delaney wanted him to go along with his shepherd and a large band of sheep into the mountains for the summer, staying in the very regions Muir wished to explore. He wished Muir simply to see that the shepherd did his duties, and be on hand in any emergency. He would be free to roam the mountains and study plants all he wished. This seemed like a splendid arrangement and Muir accepted the job.

Before they left for the mountains, one of Muir's friends there, who had a very intelligent and useful dog, came to see him. He feared the summer heat would be the death of the dog and asked Muir to take him along into the mountains, saying that he would find him very intelligent and loyal. Muir called the dog, Carlo, to him and asked him if he was willing to go with him. The dog seemed to understand and looked at his master who nodded and waved at Muir. Thereafter he was Muir's constant companion.

In June the band of 2,050 sheep started for the mountains, traveling at the rate of about a mile an hour. Mr. Delaney led the way with pack-horses carrying provisions and camp equipment. Muir's nickname for Delaney was Don Quixote. With the sheep came Billy, the shepherd, with a Chinaman and a Digger Indian to assist him for awhile, and Muir. The little lambs grew weary with travel on the warm days, but a night's rest and refreshment restored them to vigor. The men helped themselves to the hot camp food, pork and beans, bread and coffee, sat about the fire in conversation for some time, then rolled into their blankets and slept.

After breakfast each day they were quickly on the march. The brown, brushy foothills afforded little food for the sheep, and made weary travel. But soon they reached Brown's Flat above Coulterville with its green pastures and the sheep were content. Sometimes they ate some of the azalea leaves which made them very sick. These June days were filled with glorious sunshine and all about were robins, orioles, tanagers, flitting and singing. Muir was filled with happiness. He exclaimed: "Oh, these vast, calm, measureless mountain days . . . equally divine, opening a thousand windows to show us God."

Muir became acquainted here with the red ants and big jet-black ants with a bite that made one jump with pain. Scampering about camp and in the forests were the gray and the Douglas squirrels, beautiful creatures. The Douglas was his favorite, "a hot spark of life, full of scolding, brag, and fight." Muir never tired watching his antics. Along the streams he found a strange bird, wading and diving into the water for its food though evidently not a water-bird. Muir later learned that it was called the water ouzel or dipper. It became his favorite bird.

The stream and pool banks were covered with masses of ferns and among them the stately and beautiful Washington lily. Now and then his nature travel was interrupted by troubles with the sheep. One night three hundred sheep were missing. Since the shepherd had to stay with the main band, it became Muir's task to find the lost ones. With his dog, Carlo, who could follow them by scent, he soon found them in an open space among chaparral, huddled together, "as if afraid of their freedom." Muir said of the dog, "No friend and helper could be more affectionate and constant than Carlo, . . . an honor to his race."

About the middle of June Mr. Delaney returned to his valley ranch, promising to bring up supplies in two weeks. But he was delayed until July 7th, and the camp had run out of flour, beans and coffee. All hands were living on mutton which they choked down with difficulty. "At last Don Delaney came doon the lang glen" and all rejoiced. The band of sheep were moved up the mountain ridge, halting a night at Hazel Green, and other nights at Crane Flat and Tamarack Flat. Parties of Yosemite tourists, dressed in gaudy attire and mounted on mustang ponies, passed them at these points.

It was Delaney's plan to locate another permanent camp on Yosemite Creek a mile or two above the Falls. The clear, swift-flowing stream was about forty feet wide at the crossing, but the sheep would not enter the water. They took a mother across, then leaders across, then pushed a bunch of them into the stream, but all fought to go back to the whole band. After struggling all day, the men were about to quit for the night when suddenly an old sheep plunged into the water and swam across. Immediately all the sheep followed, trampling each other in the stream, yet fortunately none was drowned. No sooner had all crossed than they quieted down and began cropping the

75

tender grass as though nothing unusual had happened.

Muir was now foot-free in the country of his heart's desire. A wonderland of peaks, domes, canyons, came into view, beyond "the most extravagant description." As he rambled along the Yosemite walls above the Valley he was fairly overcome with awe and rejoicing in its grandeur. He wrote: "I shouted and gesticulated in a wild burst of ecstasy, much to the astonishment of Carlo." A brown bear, feeding nearby, ran away in fright. Continuing from point to point he came to the top of Yosemite Falls and crept down the stream's smooth course to the very brink. For the last few feet beside the dashing water, he removed his shoes and slid down to a rim-rock on the edge against which he could lodge his feet. Then he raised himself to a sitting position and peaked over the brim. The sudden shock of the vast depth below him dazed him for a moment and he laid himself back on the rock. Recovering his equilibrium he scanned the marvelous scenery for hours. But that night he awoke, again and again feeling that he was falling over the brink of the Falls. The next day on a stroll with Carlo, he found a giant bear in a thicket, and, unaware of Muir's presence, it continued feeding. John thought he would see how fast a bear could run when frightened, so he shouted and ran toward him. But the bear merely turned and stared at him. Muir halted with alarm, but stood his ground until the bear in apparent unconcern ambled away.

In camp Muir was amused at the pants which Billy the shepherd wore and never changed. He carried his noon lunch of beans and fat pork in a little bag tied to his belt.

The drippings collected on his pant legs and gathered dirt, leaves, and disintegrated rock until they could stand alone. Muir said that they represented a cross-section of nature around them.

The summer days were filled with glorious sunshine, and sometimes with cloudlands of magnificent formations. There would come the flash of lightning, crash of thunder, torrents of rain, and all the landscape would reappear refreshed and clean. The great polished dome of Mt. Hoffman and the glaciated, rock-bound Lake Tenaya exhibited to Muir a story of ice carving through geological ages. Often he wandered into these wilds with a piece of dry bread, a cup, a little tea and some matches. If overtaken by night, he would make camp in some juniper grove, eat his bread with a cup of hot tea and lie down to pleasant slumber.

On a late afternoon in August Muir was on North Dome sketching the landscape when there came to him a strange impression that his friend, Prof. Butler of Wisconsin University was in the Valley below. He could not shake off the premonition. He had known that Prof. Butler would visit California that summer, but did not suppose they could meet in this wilderness. Nevertheless he started down the precipitous Indian Creek Canyon to the Valley floor, then recalled that it would be late in the evening before he could find the hotel and perhaps everybody would be asleep. So he turned back.

But the next morning the idea still in his mind, he hurried down into the Valley and inquired whether a Prof. Butler had registered there. They replied that such was the case and that he had arrived the prior afternoon, which was the very time Muir had become conscious of his presence. The party was then on a trip to Vernal and Nevada Falls. Muir set out at once to overtake them. He was dressed in a clean pair of overalls, a cashmere shirt, and a jacket, the best outfit in his mountain wardrobe. At the foot of Vernal Falls Muir met a member of the Butler party, General Alvord, who was greatly surprised when Muir inquired for Dr. Butler, as he supposed no one knew that the professor was in the Valley.

Being informed that Dr. Butler was on the trail above the Falls Muir hastened on and found him sitting on a rock wiping perspiration from his face. He said, "Professor Butler, don't you know me." Butler replied, "I think not." Then with sudden recognition he cried, "John Muir, John Muir, where have you come from?" Explanations followed and all returned to the hotel for dinner and an evening of conversation. Muir's premonition of Dr. Butler's presence in the Valley became the talk of all the Yosemite visitors.

In early August Don Delaney moved his band of sheep on up the ridge, passing beautiful Lake Tenaya, and located a new base camp on the Tuolumne Meadows. Here the sheep were content with green pastures and Muir was thrilled with its surrounding peaks, lakes, gorges, magnificent forests and flowery meadows. In a nook at the base of Cathedral Peak he found a specimen of little Cassiope, the first he had seen and which became his best loved flower.

While the sheep camp was on Tuolumne Meadows near the lower Soda Springs, Muir made a trip over Mono Pass, down Bloody Canyon to the desert region and weird Mono Lake. He spent a cold, windy night on a rocky shelf in the canyon, and on the next day met a band of Mono Indians on their way to the Yosemite to gather acorns. They gathered around Muir begging for tobacco and whisky, and were much disappointed when he could give them none. At the foot of the Pass in a moist area he found lilies taller than his head. And nearby was a patch of wild rye which Indian women were harvesting. He visited the Mono Craters and the desolate Mono Lake which he found very interesting in spite of hot sand and sun.

But John was glad to get back to the green fields and shady forests of the Tuolumne. Late August days, cool, bright, sparkling, with shifting clouds, were now with them. It was Indian Summer but the mornings were frosty and invigorating. Muir planned one last exploratory trip, climbing many of the high peaks along the crest of the range.

In early September Mr. Delaney arrived at the Tuolumne Meadow camp to take the sheep back to the San Joaquin Valley ranch. A premature autumn storm could do much damage to the band. On September ninth, the men with pack-horses, equipment and the sheep, moved slowly down the trail homeward. They rested a night at each of their old campgrounds at Tenaya Lake, Yosemite Creek, Cascade Creek, Tamarack Flat, Crane Flat, Hazel Green, and Brown's Flat, reaching Delaney's place on September 21st.

Of the two thousand and fifty sheep that left for the mountains in the spring, two thousand and twenty-five returned, fat and healthy. Ten had been killed by bears, one by a rattlesnake, one had to be killed after breaking its leg and one was lost in the wilds. Of the remaining twelve, three had been sold to ranchers on the road, and nine had been butchered for food. Thus all were accounted for, a good record.

CHAPTER SEVEN

YOSEMITE EXPLORATIONS

During eight weeks of the autumn of 1869, John Muir worked for Mr. Delaney, breaking horses to harness, building fences and operating a gang-plow. He learned that his University of Wisconsin friends, Prof. and Mrs. Ezra S. Carr, had been transferred to the University of California at Berkeley. Mrs. Carr sent him an invitation to visit them in their new home, but Muir insisted that his Yosemite Mountains were calling him back where he might listen "to the winter songs and sermons preached and sung only there." Thus in mid-November he set out on foot for the Valley by way of Pino Blanco, Coulterville, and Harding's Mill.

Few people had braved the winter storms in the Yosemite Valley prior to this time. James C. Lamon had visited there in 1857 and became its first all year resident in 1862. J. M. Hutchings and wife settled there in 1864. Muir now, in December of 1869, joined them and wrote to Mrs. Carr, "Just think of the grandeur of a mountain winter in Yosemite," and added, "You speak of dying and going to the woods. I am dead and gone to Heaven."

By a fortunate arrangement with Mr. Hutchings, Muir was employed to set up and operate a sawmill. A previous winter storm had blown down numerous pine trees which could be sawed into lumber needed for Hutchings' resort buildings. Hutchings' house, which served also as a hotel, stood on the south side of the river near the foot of Sentinel

Peak. Muir built a little shakes cabin for himself on the north side near the Lower Yosemite Falls, and dug a little ditch by which he brought a stream of water to, and through, the cabin. Inside he planted ferns by a window where friendly frogs would chirp to him and the little stream sing for him in the evenings. He boarded with the Hutchings. Mail was carried in and out of the Valley by Indian Tom. So John was all set for a glorious winter, sawing lumber on week days and hiking into the Sierras on Sundays, "screaming among the peaks and outside meadows like a Negro Methodist in revival time."

With spring and summer came visitors to the Valley, about fifty in May. To Mrs. Carr he wrote that she need not fear that they would desecrate its beauty, saying that they "float slowly about the bottom of the Valley as a harmless scum . . . leaving the rocks and falls as eloquent as ever." Among them Muir met some famous visitors, President Mark Hopkins of Williams College in Massachusetts, and Prof. Joseph Le Conte and his troop of ten University of California boys making a geological tour of the Sierras. Prof. Le Conte described this tour later in a charming booklet, "Ramblings through the high Sierras of California by the University Excursion Party."

Muir accepted Prof. Le Conte's invitation to go with them and joined their exploring trip for several days. In a letter to Mrs. Carr, he gave a brief account of their excursions. Their first camp was at Eagle Point overlooking the Valley, the whole landscape "silvered by the moon." The second camp was at Lake Tenaya where he and Prof. Le Conte sat on glaciated rocks and discussed during many moonlit hours the story of the Sierras and their ancient glaciers. The third camp was on the gentian meadows of the Tuolumne near the lower Soda Springs. They were among "spirey mountain peaks" in an "alpine heaven." The fourth camp was among huge rocks in a rain storm at the foot of Mt. Dana. Then they descended Bloody Canyon amid flower gardens and dashing cascades, and by night reached Mono Lake where their delightful fellowship came to a close. The next day Le Conte's party went on to Lake Tahoe, and Muir visited and climbed one of the Mono Craters, then returned to his Yosemite cabin.

In this summer of 1870 Therese Yelverton, a fiction writer, visited the Yosemite Valley and became so interested in a number of striking individuals there, that she composed a novel about them entitled Zanita. Muir, the Hutchings and their daughters, Florence and Cosa, played principal parts. Florence, a handsome and mischievous topsy, was Zanita, and Cosa was a very precious darling of a child. Muir, she described as wearing soiled, ragged clothing, but usually adorned by a bunch of ferns or flowers. She represented him as having "open, blue eyes, his bright, intelligent face shining with a pure and holy enthusiasm." She pictured him as a "lithe figure . . . skipping over rough boulders . . . skirting a shelf or rock with the cautious activity of a goat."

That fall of 1870 Mr. Hutchings requested the use of Muir's cabin for his sister, and during this period of some weeks, Muir worked again for Mr. Delaney on the valley ranch near Snelling. But in the winter he was back at his sugar pine cabin spending the long winter evenings beside his cozy fireplace, reading books of Von Humboldt, Lyell, Tyndall, Darwin, and late botanical works. Letters to his sister, Sarah, and to Mrs. Carr were usually headed, "In the Sawmill, Yosemite Valley." He would remark, "It is hard to write here as the mill jars so much by the stroke of the saw, and the rain drips from the roof, and I have to set the log every few minutes. . . . I like the piney fragrance of the fresh-sawn boards. . . . I sleep in the mill for the sake of hearing the murmuring hush of the water beneath me . . . and I have a small, box-like home fastened beneath the gable of the mill, looking westward down the valley . . . people call it the hang-nest, because it seems unsupported."

One moonlight evening in springtime Muir noticed that a wind was pushing the upper Yosemite Falls away from the wall back of it. There was a narrow ledge on the face of the wall by which he thought he could climb behind the falling torrent and witness innumerable rainbows displayed in the moonlight. In a short time he had climbed to the ledge and crept out upon it. The view of millions of sparkling, colored drops of water was glorious beyond expectation. But suddenly the wind died away and the crashing waterfall beat upon him like millions of tiny pebbles. He clung to his precarious perch until fortunately the wind shifted the Falls out again and he quickly retreated, wet, sore and cold, to his warm cabin.

In the month of May, 1871, Ralph Waldo Emerson visited the Yosemite with a notable party of friends. People at the hotel would remark in admiring whispers, "Emerson is here." Shy John Muir only hovered on the far rim of the admiring circle. But he did make bold to leave a note for Emerson at the hotel. The famous man inquired for Muir and went to the mill to meet him. During the next few days they spent many hours together in Muir's hang-nest at the mill discussing the wonders of the Yosemite region. When Emerson left the Valley to visit the Mariposa Grove of Big Trees, he invited Muir to go with his party. Muir suggested that they camp there for a night which Emerson accepted with pleasure. But the cautious friends, fearing for his health, vetoed the plan. Muir described their parting: "I followed to the edge of the Grove. Emerson lingered in the rear of the train, and when he reached the top of the ridge, after all of the rest of the party were over and out of sight, he turned his horse, took off his hat and waved me a last good-bye."

In the summer of 1871 Muir quit his work at the sawmill. It became apparent that Hutchings was displeased with Muir's growing popularity among the visitors, who turned to him for information rather than to Hutchings. To the crowd Hutchings was just a good hotel keeper, but Muir was a charming individual and a nature authority. In making the change Muir was evidently more influenced by his desire to give more time to his glacial studies. The State Geologist, J. D. Whitney, had published his conclusions regarding the origin of the Valley arguing that it was caused by an ancient cataclysmic sinking of the floor between the adjoining walls. John Muir held a new theory that in the ice age, vast glaciers had ploughed out these canyons, aided by water erosion. Prof. Le Conte had agreed with him in this view.

Muir, in his explorations of the mountain regions above the Valley, had discovered a number of residual glaciers, still many hundreds of feet thick, lying on the flanks of the mountains. He traced five of these great glaciers, showing how they had carved out and polished the gorges descending into the main Yosemite. These glaciers were the Yosemite Creek, the Hoffman, the Tenaya, the South Lyell, and the Illilouette. Dr. Whitney scorned these ideas as the conceptions of a mere "shepherd." However, geologists, with some reservations as to the effects of water-erosion, frost, wind and earthquakes, today agree with Muir. Mrs. Carr thought Muir was spending too much time on such projects, but he replied: "You speak heresy for once, and deserve a dip in Methodist Tophet . . . I have just been sending ice to Le Conte, and snow to McChesney, and I have nothing left but hailstones for you." [The writer, a Methodist minister, fully appreciates these sly digs!]

John Muir, on leaving Hutchings' employment, took up quarters at Black's Hotel near the foot of Cathedral Peaks. In the following winter he was in charge of the premises and had much extra time for nature studies and writing. In the late fall he made "a last raid of the season," outfitted with a pair of blankets and a quantity of bread and coffee. He explored the Hetch Hetchy Valley and the Grand Canyon of the Tuolumne. To his mother he wrote: "Between two and three thousand persons visited the Valley this summer. I am glad they are all gone. I can now think my thoughts and say my prayers in quiet."

In the winter of 1871-72 Muir began to write for publication. His first articles, Yosemite Glaciers, Yosemite Winter, and Yosemite Spring, were published in the New York Daily Tribune, and attracted wide attention. Then he began a series of articles for the Overland Monthly, the journal founded by Bret Harte. Two of these were Yosemite Valley in Flood and Twenty Hill Hollow. Later in this Journal appeared the interesting series: Mountain

Sculptor, Origin of Yosemite Valleys, Ancient Glaciers and Their Pathways, Glacial Denudation, Formation of Soils, and Mountain Building. To Muir writing was tedious work, but he was reaching a large public and reaping financial reward.

Two friends of these Yosemite years were the actor, Henry Edwards, and J. B. McChesney of Oakland. When Muir was away in the mountains without access to authoritative books, these friends would identify plants and insects for him. Edwards had one of the finest collections of butterflies and beetles in the world. Muir made a collection of Yosemite butterflies for him which had four species new to Edwards and two new to science.

Early in the morning of March 26th, 1872, a great earthquake shook the Yosemite region, sending rocks crashing from the walls to the Valley floor. Muir was awakened from sleep and ran out to see what caused the violent disturbance. The peaks swayed above him and the ground shook under his feet. The few white settlers in the Valley gathered at Hutchings Hotel and contemplated flight. Muir tried in vain to reassure them. The Indians along the foot of the north wall fled to the middle of the Valley in terror. As the earthquake shook the trees the birds flew out with cries of fright. Eagle Rock on the north wall a half mile up the Valley was shaken off and crashed in thousands of boulders to the floor. The roar of the earthquake was terrifying. As the worst shocks subsided, Muir hastened to the newly formed talus where the giant rocks were still shifting, grinding, and settling into place. A cloud of dust moved across the Valley sky forming a dense ceiling. All of the birds settled into a fear-bound silence except an old owl which continued his doleful hoots in apparent unconcern.

In the summer of 1872 the distinguished Harvard botanist, Asa Gray, visited the Yosemite and went botanizing with Muir, as did another famous botanist, John Torrey, a little later. In October the artist, William Keith, arrived with a letter of introduction from Mrs. Jeanne Carr, Muir's "good angel." Mrs. Carr had also put some of John's writings in the hands of the Harvard geologist, Louis Agassiz, then visiting in San Francisco. Agassiz remarked: "Muir is studying to greater purpose and with greater results than anyone else has done."

After a mid-December trip to Oakland, 1872, Muir returned to his Yosemite cabin on foot by way of Turlock, Hopeton and Coulterville. The weather was sharply cold and clear. He decided to make a mountain trip up Tenaya canyon climbing over some precipitous cliffs in what he said were the most delicate feats of mountaineering he had ever attempted. At one point in the rough gorge, he missed his footing and fell to the brink of a deep, rocky chasm, unconscious. Some brush had halted his further fall. Regaining consciousness, he quickly overcame the obstruction, ashamed of his clumsy accident. He spent two days and a night in the Canyon sketching the scenery and making notes. The third night he was at frozen Tenaya Lake, uttering his praise, "A grand old mansion is this Tenaya region." Then in a day he walked to his Yosemite cabin going down over the shoulder of Mt. Watkins to Mirror Lake, from which it was only a moonlight stroll to his door. Muir described this walk in a lengthy letter to Mrs. Carr, who without his knowledge sent it to a magazine which published it under the caption of A Geologist's Winter Walk. It is one of the finest things he ever wrote.

During the whole of August and part of September of 1873 John Muir was pursuing his studies of glaciers in the upper Yosemite region, drawing ropes taut across the ice and measuring its movement day by day. The McClure Glacier moved forty-seven inches in forty-six days and at the foot of the glacier were mounds of rock-meal, proof of glacial action.

In late September in company with Dr. A. Kellog, botanist; William Simms, artist; and Galen Clark, Guardian of the Yosemite Park, Muir made an exploring trip along the crest of the Sierras into the King's River country. The party was gone for about six weeks, covering the highest and most magnificent area of the Sierras, climbing the highest peaks, including Mt. Whitney, and exploring the deepest gorges. They dipped into the Kern River region and Owens Valley then traveled northward to Lake Tahoe, walking over a thousand wilderness miles.

After this year, 1873, Muir was no longer a resident of the Yosemite Valley, though he made frequent visits to it year after year. He now arranged to stay with his friends, the J. B. McChesneys, in Oakland, while he wrote articles for the magazines. It caused him a painful wrench of spirit to tear himself away from his beloved "Range of Light." He always carried with him in a little bag tied to his belt a note-book in which he recorded interesting incidents and discoveries. From these notes came these charming stories.

On one winter morning after a heavy snowstorm Muir left his second cabin, which stood near the foot of the Royal Arches, and started to climb a steep side canyon to the top of the Valley wall for a view of the snow-filled Yosemite and the white-robed peaks beyond. The snow was dry and fluffy and about five or six feet deep. His progress was slow and near sundown he was still several hundred feet below the summit. Suddenly his movements started an avalanche and he "was swished down to the foot of the canyon as if by enchantment." The climb up the steep ascent had taken nearly all day, but the descent occupied only a minute. Muir threw himself flat on his back with arms outstretched and coasted on his soft bed with terrific speed to the valley floor. There, uninjured, he climbed out of his fleecy bed and walked home. Of his avalanche ride he wrote: "Elijah's flight in a chariot of fire could hardly have been more gloriously exciting."

On another winter day, Muir climbed to the top of the north wall by way of Indian Creek to observe the snowy wonderland. It was a bright, sunny day with a north wind blowing. From his lofty perch he beheld hundreds of high peaks, clad in snow, and each carrying a long, fleecy banner, starting from the top of the peak and widening into the shape of a long, narrow V. They were waving in the sunlight like magnificent silk streamers. It was a beautiful spectacle.

Another strange experience came to Muir one day in late Indian summer. He had climbed to the top of Half Dome to behold the Valley and Tenaya Canyon filled with a cloud of pearly luster. "Clouds, white as snow, came from the north, trailing their downy skirts over the dark forests and entered the Valley with solemn, god-like gestures. . . ." The brilliant sun shone down on the gray surface. Suddenly he beheld that rarely observed optical phenomenon known as the "Specter of the Brocken." His shadow in clear outline of a half mile length lay on the cloud surface below him. He walked about, waving his arms and kicking his legs wildly. The shadow copied all of his antics. He never again beheld this strange phenomenon.

Muir's favorite creature in all the Sierra was the lively, acrobatic, Douglas squirrel. While wandering through the forests one day he came into an open space and sat down on a log to rest. Soon a Douglas squirrel appeared in a tall pine tree where he nimbly cut off several large pine cones. He then hurried down to the ground, gathered the cones together, and began cutting out the pine nuts. Muir watched quietly as other wild creatures came into the opening. He then began to whistle softly some old Scotch tunes such as Over the River to Charlie, Bonnie Doon, Bonnie Wood O' Craggie Dee. The wild creatures paused in their pursuits, stood motionless and listened. A bird flew within a few feet of his face, halted on wing, and peered wonderingly at him. Then Muir started the tune of Old Hundredth. Instantly there was a scream of fright, or distaste, as all scampered away to their hiding places. He tried this experiment at other times in other places, with always the same result. He had no explanation for it.

One other little creature won Muir's great affection. This was the water ouzel or dipper. The ouzel is not by nature a water bird, but by choice lives his life along water courses. He wades or darts into streams or pools for his food, builds his nest by waterfalls and enjoys the spray and water songs. Sitting on some rock or limb he utters his call with sudden lowering of his body, jerk of his head, and dip of the tail. Muir never tired of watching this charming creature.

CHAPTER EIGHT

WIDE WEST, U.S.A.

During the first eight months of the year, 1874, John Muir remained steadfastly at his desk in the home of his friends, the J. B. McChesneys, 1364 Franklin Street, Oakland. In afteryears he was accustomed to speak of that period as that "strange Oakland Epoch." It was like confinement in a prison, except for the table conversations with the family. He avoided letter writing and all social activities. His friends, especially Mrs. Carr, had been urging him to put his explorations and scientific discoveries into writing. Muir was one of the world's most brilliant conversationalists and letter writers, but book-making frightened him with its mechanics and artificiality. Yet these writings made him famous and established his authority as a naturalist.

Muir now felt that this obligation to society was satisfied. So in late September, 1874, ailing in health and harassed by the long confinement, he hurried off to his body and soul refreshing mountains. From Yosemite he wrote to Mrs. Carr: "On leaving Oakland I was so excited over my escape that . . . I forgot and left all the accounts I was to collect . . . I was in a dreamy, exhausted daze." His return to Yosemite was first by train to Turlock, then on foot into the mountains. Near Hopeton he found late autumn wildflowers still in bloom and dropping his coat and shirt by the wayside, he crept joyously among them, remarking: "I was wild once more and let my watch warn and point as it pleased." On the sands he observed beautiful little tracks, like embroidery. A diligent search revealed them to be the footprints of lizards, grasshoppers, mice and birds. That evening he visited his friend Delaney at his ranch. During the following autumn days he passed leisurely through mountain scenery at Coulterville, Bower Cave, Hazel Green, Crane's Flat and down into "the groves and meadows of Yosemite."

Muir said that he felt like a stranger there as he had come to say good-bye. But his leave-taking was postponed for several weeks. He revisited the delightful places where in company with Mrs. Carr and Emily Pelton he had gone the year before. Then he crossed the range to Mono Lake and walked northward to Lake Tahoe. For some reason the editors of his papers made little use of his Tahoe notes. Yet he visited the region many times and the few references taken from his notes reveal his great interest in the area, probably second only to the Yosemite.

Muir now hurried up the Sacramento Valley following the old stage road to Sisson and Mt. Shasta. There he sought in vain for a companion with whom to climb the great peak. All insisted that it was too late in the season, an early storm would make the trip very dangerous. However, a mountain guide, Jerome Fay, took him and his camp equipment on pack horses to the timberline shelter. The next day, alone, he climbed to the mountain top, rejoicing in the vast sweep of glorious landscape that met his eyes. But an approaching storm made him hasten back to his timberline camp before dark. Here with firewood, food and shelter, he watched the storm rage about him for five days. He studied snowflakes with a lens, observed squirrels digging out their hidden stores and wild sheep taking shelter near his camp. He was really disappointed when Mr. Sisson arrived with horses to take him back to town.

In the next few weeks of mostly calm, sunny weather, Muir wandered around the base of the great mountain, a distance of about a hundred miles. The forests, gorges, glaciers, streams, flowery meadows, were an unfailing delight to him. His letters describing his journey were published in the San Francisco Evening Bulletin to the great pleasure of its readers. One fascinating spot was the headwaters of the McCloud River, which began in a spring "fifty yards wide at the mouth, issuing from the base of a lava bluff . . . from a world of ferns and mosses, gold and green."

In late December he returned to the Sacramento Valley by stage and train, going to Brownsville in the foothills between the Yuba and Feather Rivers to visit his friend, Emily Pelton. While there a great storm struck the region flooding the Sacramento Valley. It lasted for days, in one of which Muir ventured forth to view the storm beating upon the forested ridges. For hours he wandered afield, drenched and driven by wind and rain. Often he was forced to seek shelter behind some tree or rock in order to catch his breath and rest from the violence of the storm. Then on a high hill a notion occurred to him to climb to the top of a tall spruce tree which was swaying from side to side almost touching the ground at each swing. Muir reached the tree top and for two hours hung on for one of the strangest experiences of his life. Few people would have wished or dared to take such a ride.

When he returned to the Pelton home they commiserated him upon his soiled, soaked, and bedraggled appearance, but he assured them that he had spent a most enjoyable day in the wild storm. This incident was described in his book, The Mountains of California, and has always been a favorite story among his readers.

In April, 1875, Muir went back to Mt. Shasta with a Coast and Geodetic Survey party to put an elevation marker there. Two days later he made another ascent of the mountain with Jerome Fay to complete some barometrical observations. A sudden storm of wind, snow and hail broke upon them. Unable to reach their timberline camp, they huddled about one of the steaming fumeroles at the summit during the night. In the morning, weak, stiff and almost frozen, they managed to stumble back to the timberline camp. Muir described this incident as "one of the most violent snowstorms imaginable." He wrote—"I am scarred and battered like a log that has come down the Tuolumne in flood time." Yet he insisted that he had a "very instructive and delightful trip."

In this summer, 1875, Muir, with his friends, William Keith, J. B. McChesney, and John Swett, made a tour of the high Sierras from the Yosemite to Mt. Whitney. On this and a later trip that summer, Muir was observing what damage sawmills and fires started by sheep men were causing to the forests. This frightful loss was called to the attention of the Legislature but in vain. On these enjoyable travel days, John Swett kept reminding Muir of his writing responsibilities, and Muir remarked: "John Swett, who is brother now, papa then, orders me home to booking. Bless me, what an awful thing town duty is."

That winter of 1875-76 Muir stayed at the San Francisco home of John Swett at 1419 Taylor Street. Swett, a brilliant educator, is remembered as the Father of the Public School System in California. In this congenial atmosphere Muir continued his writing and lecturing, both distasteful work to him. But he remarked: "I always make out to accomplish in some way what I undertake." Muir did his writing with a quill pen which he cut for himself. The one he was then using came from the wing of a golden eagle which he picked up on Mt. Hoffman. Sometimes, he admitted, he used a feather from "some old gray goose."

In 1875 John's friend, Prof. Carr, was elected State Superintendent of Education and Mrs. Carr served as deputy in the office at Sacramento. During this period the Carrs bought some land near Los Angeles and established a home there under the name of "Carmelito," which for a time became a literary center of the State. Helen Hunt Jackson wrote part of her famous novel Ramona there. To the spacious grounds Muir donated many plants, shrubs and trees.

In the spring of 1877 Muir made an excursion into Utah, much of it around the great Salt Lake and the City of the Saints. Regarding his travels he wrote four interesting letters, later included in his book, Steep Trails. These were: The City of the Saints; A Great Storm in Utah; Bathing in Salt Lake; and Mormon Lilies. Of Salt Lake City he commented: "At first sight there is nothing very marked in the external appearance of the town excepting its leafiness." The houses were built of bluish-gray adobe brick, surrounded by flower gardens of lilacs and tulips, "artless and humble." At the side or rear were thrifty orchards. The people, he thought, had a weary, depressed look, especially the ones from the country. He often heard the remark: "We saints are not as bad as we are called." Muir thought them friendly and charitable.

The second letter described a great storm, May 18th, which broke over the city in spectacular cloud formations, pushing waves of dust like enormous sea-combers. Torrential rain and snow followed. "The crystal flakes falling in the foul streets was a pitiful sight."

In his third letter Muir described a swim he took in the great Salt Lake. "I sauntered along the shore until I came to a sequestered cove where buttercups and wild peas were blooming. . . . Here, I thought, is just the place for a bath." But the waves were so big and threatening, that he gave up the idea, only to return an hour later and take the plunge. He ducked under an oncoming wave and sped away glad and free on a joyous ride, lifted on the shoulders of the buoyant bouncing waters. He said it was the most exciting swim he had taken west of the Rockies.

The fourth letter concerned the flower gardens in the green nooks of the Wasatch Mountains. Everywhere were ferns and orchids, violets, gilias, wallflowers, smilax, and miles of blooming bushes. But his most interesting discovery was of some cloistered gardens at the foot of some cliffs within a few feet of snow banks, where hundreds of lilies grew, not in masses but in roomy separation. The winds tossed their blossoms and seemed to ring their dainty bells on the breeze.

Muir returned to California in July and made a brief excursion into the Yosemite again, reporting to Mrs. Carr: "I never enjoyed the Tuolumne cataracts so much; coming out of the sun lands and the gray salt deserts of Utah, these wild ice waters sang themselves into my soul more enthusiastically than ever."

In the latter part of July Muir sailed from San Francisco to Los Angeles, spending several weeks in the San Gabriel Valley and the San Gabriel Mountains. At Pasadena he found Dr. E. M. Conger, who had been a fellow student at the University of Wisconsin. Conger owned an orange orchard in the San Gabriel Valley to which he took Muir, telling him of the beauty of his place and the enormous profit in orange growing. He also grew lemon and lime trees. Muir said he was tempted to buy an orchard and settle down there. But the mountains were calling again and he turned his steps into the rugged, thorny San Gabriels. The range was about forty miles long by about half that width. It extended from Cajon Pass to the Santa Monica Coast Mountains. For five days he hiked over rocky ridges and through miles of chaparral thickets exploring hill and valley toward the sea. At a little secluded pool where birds came to drink, he suddenly noticed a rattle-snake lying between his feet. Muir, "lifting his foot a little higher than usual" stepped away permitting the snake to glide into the brush in peace. It was the snake's abode, he said.

Muir visited the Carrs' Pasadena Patch but found that they were away from home. The next day, August 13th, he took a train for Monterey, where he rambled over the hills and through forests to Santa Cruz and then over the range to San Jose. There, while visiting friends, he climbed Mt. Hamilton.

Arriving home Muir found an invitation awaiting him to guide two famous botanists, Sir Joseph Hooker of Eng-

99

land, and Prof. Asa Gray of Harvard, on a botanical expedition up the Sacramento Valley to the glorious flower gardens on the flanks of Mt. Shasta. This was a high compliment to Muir, and he thoroughly enjoyed exploring the country with two such specialists and treasured the memory of conversations around the evening campfires. One evening on the slope of Mt. Shasta Asa Gray spoke of a charming little evergreen plant—linnaea borealis, saying that it was strange that Muir had never found it in California. The following day, as Hooker and Muir were botanizing along a little stream they discovered a green bank, carpeted with, of all things, linnaea! Muir thought Gray must have felt its presence the night before.

On their return trip down the Sacramento Valley they halted at the home of Gen. John Bidwell in Chico. Bidwell was a great ranch owner and also a botanical student. He conducted an experimental farm with plants imported from all over the world. General and Mrs. Bidwell were well known as gracious hosts. Inadvertently on a horseback ride, they invaded a hornet's nest which caused a hilarious flight. In a conversation with Bidwell, Muir said he hoped someday to take a canoe trip down the Sacramento River. At once Gen. Bidwell had a boat built for him. As the party separated here, Muir rowed his boat down the river.

Muir named his boat the Snag-jumper for its ability to slide over logs, roots, and other obstructions in the stream. Jumper was a curiosity and a terror to all of the birds and animals, tame or wild, along the river. They stared at it for a moment, then screamed and fled. Yet they showed no fear of passing steamers. Opposite the Sutter Buttes Muir halted and walked across the valley to climb the highest of the peaks for observations. He was back at his boat by two o'clock, a six mile walk each way.

Muir had planned on reaching the San Joaquin River to boat up that stream as far as Millerton, then make another walking tour over the rugged King's River country. But at Sacramento he discovered that portions of the San Joaquin River in this dry season were not navigable and that the distance was three hundred miles. So he left Snag-jumper there and took a steamer to San Francisco and a train to Visalia. At Hyde's Mill on the Kaweah, he obtained provisions and pushed on into the high and glorious wilderness of the Kings River country. Much of this region had been considered impassable. Muir climbed over ridges more than twelve thousand feet in altitude, making notes and measurements of cliffs, cascades, trees, and other natural objects. In one period he had only one meal in four days. His homeward journey led by Visalia, Merced, Snelling, and Hopeton, where he built a successor to Snag-jumper and rowed down to Martinez.

In a letter to his sister Sarah, November 29th, Muir referred to his visit with "my friends the Strentzels, who have eighty acres of choice orchards and vineyards." He added: "Here I rested two days, my first rest in six weeks. They pitied my weary looks, and made me eat and sleep, stuffing me with turkey and chicken, beef, fruits and jellies in the most extravagant manner imaginable, and begged me to stay a month."

His host, Dr. John Strentzel, was a native of Poland, who in youth had taken part in a revolution that failed. He escaped seizure by the Russians and fled to Hungary, where he studied viticulture and medicine at the University of

Buda-Pesth. In 1840 he emigrated to America and joined a Peter's Colonization Company which was developing lands at the site of what was later Dallas, Texas. This project failed and he moved to Lamar County, same State, where he met and married Louisiana Erwin. In 1849 as a medical advisor to the Clarksville Train of immigrants, he came to California with his wife and little daughter. Deciding that fruit growing for sale to gold miners would be more profitable than gold digging, he bought some land in Alhambra Valley near Martinez. On it he planted orchards and vineyards, and became so successful in their cultivation that he became known as the Father of Horticulture in California. The daughter, Louie Wanda, a talented and gracious young lady, had been educated at the Atkins Seminary for young ladies in Benicia. She was widely acclaimed for her love of flowers and music. Among her close friends was Mrs. Carr, the close friend also of John Muir. For several years Mrs. Carr had planned opportunities for Louie and John Muir to meet. Muir now became a frequent guest at the Strentzel home.

Muir left the Strentzel home in Alhambra Valley on a late December afternoon and climbed Mt. Diablo, reaching the top a little after dark. There he spent the night in a little nook sheltered by chaparral from a furious, cold wind. A glorious sunrise awaited him. Then he descended to the famous Mountain House where he was the only guest at breakfast. From the mountain he had a pleasant walk through the Oakland hills to the Bay.

The winter of 1877-78 Muir wrote up his travel notes for publication in newspapers and magazines, living in the home of John Swett. In early June, 1878, he was engaged by the United States Coast and Geodetic Survey to go with a party of engineers establishing a series of triangulation points along the 39th parallel across Nevada and Utah. Muir's experiences on this work with Capt. A. F. Rodgers were related in a series of letters to the Strentzel family and also in a group of articles published in the San Francisco Evening Bulletin.

Muir in a letter to the Strentzels on July 6th said that the party rode horseback to Placerville and Tahoe. The weather was very warm until they reached the Lake. They took a steamer ride around Tahoe, and also visited Cascade Lake in "three delightful days."

Their first camp was at Genoa where the rumors that Indians were on a hostile rampage were discounted. Their first triangulation point was on Grant's Peak west of Walker Lake. Here Muir found some Nevada prunes with a fine wild flavor which he sent to Dr. Strentzel suggesting that he plant the seed to see what could be done with them. This letter was mailed from Wellington on the West Walker River near the interesting Wilson Canyon dear to rock-hounds.

The next station was Austin which they reached by way of the old Buckland Pony Express Station and old Fort Churchill, crossing a number of desert ranges. Of this trip Muir exclaimed: "Boo! how hot it was riding in the solemn, silent glare, shadeless, waterless." One day they ran into a cloudburst and were pelted with hailstones. The cloud-drapery, blue-sky windows, and the lightning made a most impressive picture. Late in August the party moved to Belmont, then county seat of Nye County, a town of 4,000 people. Today it lies in ruin, uninhabited, desolate. Muir's letter from Belmont described a serious experience of the party on Lone Mountain where Muir's endurance and desert skill saved them. Muir managed to get the men, delirious and barely alive, to a water-hole on the morning of the third day.

The next base camp was at Hamilton where the group was stationed for several weeks. Hamilton some years previous had a population of eight to ten thousand people. The neighboring towns—Treasury City, perhaps seven thousand; Shermantown, six thousand; and Swansea, three thousand. Muir reported that at this time these were already deserted towns with only a handful of people in any of them. Triangulation work accomplished here, the party moved on to a brief stop at Ward Mine, south of Ely. They arrived after dark and pitched camp in a corral atop a windy hill. A gale soon struck them, blowing alkali and ammonia dust into eyes, ears and everything. They managed to collect their gear, find a room in the little mining village where they could wash and comb themselves to comfort and decency. After a few more days' work the party completed its summer work and returned to San Francisco.

John Muir's five articles, which were later included in his book, Steep Trails, are summarized briefly here. They were originally published in the San Francisco Evening Bulletin, and were headed Nevada Farms, Nevada Forests, Nevada Timber Belt, Glacial Phenomena in Nevada, and Nevada's Dead Towns. Farms in Nevada, Muir decided, would, with only exceptions of fertile oases, have a hard, uphill struggle against desert sand, sage, and burning sun. The pioneer farmers, he said, were plodding Dutchmen, living content in the desert hills and valleys. For awhile rich mine markets made them prosperous. However there were some rare exceptions.

In the matter of Nevada forests Muir said that the State had about sixty-five mountain ranges, every one of which had groves of coniferous trees, four pines, two spruces, two Junipers and one fir—in variety. The principal lumber trees of Nevada are the white pine, fox-tail pine and the Douglas spruce. Perhaps, he said, the most interesting tree and most valuable to the Indian population was the nut pine, which in normal seasons, he insisted, provided a crop of nuts greater than the entire wheat crop of California. The Indian families gather the nuts as their staff of life. Whole tribes assemble with beating poles, baskets, bags, and camp-gear for the harvest. The evenings are times of fun and frolic around a campfire for old and young.

In Muir's explorations in Nevada, he found evidence of glacial action all over the state. From his studies he formed four generalizations regarding it. First: the Great Basin was originally an elevated tableland, bald and featureless, not broken into ranges and valleys as today. Second: this tableland was bounded on the east and west by high mountain ranges, but open at the north and south to vast ice flows that gouged out the long valleys and canyons which today lie north-south. Third: as the ice age terminated, the water collected in the low valleys forming lakes, into which side glaciers from the ranges worked down digging out the numerous east-west gorges or little valleys of the present. Fourth: the few great lakes gradually dried up leaving vast, sandy, sage plains or alkali flats.

Muir's concluding article on Nevada concerned its "dead towns." Nevada, one of the youngest of our States, yet is everywhere strewn with silent, crumbling ruins like that of an ancient civilization. In a little canyon near Austin, he found five uninhabited villages, their very names and purpose forgotten. In the big Smoky Valley, south of Austin, Muir saw a tall smokestack built of solid masonry and standing in solitary grandeur at the mouth of a dry gulch. He said it looked like someone had moved it out there and left it by mistake. It had been built by a New York Company to smelt ore which they hoped to find, but never did. These scores of dead towns in the desert ranges of Nevada, he said, "waste in the dry wilderness like the bones of cattle that have died of thirst."

When Muir returned to San Francisco in the fall of 1878, he found that Mrs. Swett was very ill, so he took up lodgings in the home of another friend, a Mr. Isaac Upham, a book-seller, who lived at 920 Valencia Street. Here he settled down to writing many articles for the San Francisco Evening Bulletin, and the Harper's and Scribner's Magazines. It was always dull, tedious work for him, but it brought in a steady income and increasing fame. It was noticeable however, through the winter months, that Muir often slipped away from the city for frequent visits to the Strentzel home in Alhambra Valley near Martinez. It was strange that even close friends did not suspect the real reason for the calls.

CHAPTER NINE

ALASKA TRAVELS

Early in the year of 1879 Muir planned to tour the Puget Sound region and probably go north to Alaska. In the meantime his visits to the Strentzel home in Alhambra Valley became more frequent, and the friendship with Miss Louie Wanda Strentzel culminated in a marriage engagement. They were admirably suited to each other. And apparently there was a complete understanding and agreement between them regarding Muir's many and long exploration trips which were his life interest and work. Their engagement, however, was kept a close secret from everyone except Dr. and Mrs. Strentzel, Louie's parents. Even Mrs. Carr, who had planned and hoped for this happy event, did not learn of it for several months.

Muir sailed from San Francisco for the north country around Puget Sound in early May of 1879 and reached Esquimault Harbor, near Victoria, at the southern end of Vancouver Island. With Victoria as his base he made many short trips into the sourrounding region—Nanaimo, Burrard Inlet, Fraser River, etc., charmed, as he said, "with the wild, new-born scenery." Most interesting of all were the wonderful forested areas along Puget Sound to Port Townsend, Seattle, Olympia, and Tacoma. The long finger of the sound, reaching to Olympia with still, clear water and forested shore, reminded him of Lake Tahoe. All of the towns, he said, had a hopeful, thrifty aspect. Muir obtained glorious views of Mounts Baker, Adams,

St. Helens, Hood, and grandest of all, Mount Rainier, directly east of Seattle. He visited Rainier, wishing that he might climb it, but his time schedule forced him to wait till a later occasion.

After a few weeks, an all too brief period, Muir sailed from Portland, Oregon on the mail steamer, California, for Alaska. They went down the broad Columbia River, called at Port Townsend and Victoria, then northward into quiet, inland waters, passing numerous wooded islands which gave one the feeling of floating through a fairyland. The days were clear and calm and the breezes cool and refreshing. On July 14th the ship reached Ft. Wrangell, halting only a few hours, and going on to Sitka, then back to Ft. Wrangell by the 20th. The steamer then returned to San Francisco, taking along Muir's friend who had accompanied him on his excursions so far. Muir said he watched the ship depart with a very lonesome feeling. Ft. Wrangell was a dreary, slovenly built village, standing on boggy ground without a tavern or lodging house in it. Muir walked about its streets, pondering his predicament, when he met one of the Presbyterian missionaries, Dr. Sheldon Jackson, who invited him to sleep in their carpenter shop. Muir hastened to get his bags and slept there one night, when a better fortune overtook him. A merchant, a Mr. Vanderbilt, heard of his glacial interests and homeless situation and kindly invited him to a room in his home and a place at his table. Mr. Vanderbilt introduced him to the prospectors and traders and head men of the Indian tribe. Muir's explorations in the country among trees, stumps, bushes, aroused the curiosity of both whites and Indians who kept "wondering what he was up to."

Then one of Muir's experiments caused fright and con-
sternation in the village. One night in the midst of a great
rainstorm, he climbed over the hill back of the town to
listen to the song of the trees as they were swayed by the
gale. To observe their motions he started a little fire and
kept building it up until he had a flame leaping many feet
into the air, throwing brilliant colors upon the clouds. In
town some Indians saw the strange lights and with wild
alarm begged the collector of customs to ask the missionaries to pray away the frightful omen. The fire behind
the hill could not be seen, but the magnificent spectacle on
the clouds was awesome and vastly disturbing to Indians
and whites alike. They had never seen anything like it
before. Was it a volcano, or St. Elmo's fire, or, as the Indians feared, the work of an evil god? Muir said that of all
his thousands of campfires this was the most triumphant
and storm-defying in grandeur.

Wrangell Island, narrow and about fourteen miles long,
was separated from the mainland by a forested shoreline.
The village and fort had been a government station, now
released to private ownership. Its business depended on
the Cassier gold mines, a hundred and fifty to two hundred
miles up the Stickeen River. The town was strangely quiet
and peaceful, no brawls in the streets. The rains and the
sea were calm and gentle. There were no horses on the
island and only a few chickens, sheep, and hogs. The old
square fort was occupied by the Presbyterian mission. The
common mode of travel was by canoe. The woods and
meadows were full of berries, huckleberries, salmonberries,
blackberries, raspberries, serviceberries and cranberries, in
vast abundance. Muir went along with a party into these

109

berry patches under the guidance of the Collector, and while the Indians gathered fruit he botanized in the sphagnum and carex bogs which were similar to those in Wisconsin and Canada. Everywhere among the Indian people there was kindliness and serene good nature. The tribe adopted Muir and gave him an Indian name, which the Presbyterian missionaries said would be a safeguard in travel among Indians of any tribe.

One evening the Stickeen tribe gave the missionaries and Muir a reception at Chief Skake's blockhouse, providing a dinner and performing dances and imitations of animals. This was followed by speeches of welcome to the missionaries and a potlatch in which robes made of animal skins, and fantastic headgear, were given to all, including Muir.

Near Ft. Wrangell the Stickeen River reaches the sea. It starts far inland, travels three hundred and fifty miles—one hundred of which is in a canyon cut through the Coast Range, three to five thousand feet deep. At intervals along these canyon walls are numerous great glaciers and waterfalls. This stream, navigable for one hundred and fifty miles, was followed by the miners to the gold fields far inland. Shortly after his arrival in Ft. Wrangell, Muir took a boat ride up the River with the Presbyterian missionaries to the head of navigation at Glenora, a town at the foot of Glenora Peak. On the way they passed the two largest glaciers, the Stickeen and the Dirt. The ship captain announced that he would leave for home the next morning.

It was then 1 P.M. Glenora Peak was famous for its magnificent view and Muir felt that he could climb it and return by dark. Dr. S. Hall Young, one of the missionaries, asked permission to go along. Muir pointed out that it would be a trip of about fourteen miles through brush, over boulders, and up a steep ascent of seven thousand feet, a severe task for a seasoned mountaineer. But Dr. Young insisted that he was a strong walker and climber and would be no trouble. He proved his ability to take care of himself as they climbed the peak. But near the top they reached a perpendicular and disintegrating wall of rock. Muir in the lead, called to Dr. Young a little distance behind, warning him that the rock was dangerous. A few moments later there was a scream for help. Muir hastened back and found Dr. Young lying face down in a little gully on the edge of a thousand foot drop. Only a few slender bushes had stopped his fall. His arms had been dislocated, making him helpless. Muir, clinging to the precipitous wall with one hand, carried Dr. Young by the coat collar in the other hand back to a little ledge in safety. How he did that was a mystery, even to him. There he examined the slope for a possible route of escape, and decided that his best course was down the steep gully to the top of the glacier. Tying Dr. Young's useless arms to his body with his suspenders, Muir supported him, notch by notch cut in the gully wall, until by midnight he reached the bottom. There he pulled one of Dr. Young's arms back into place, but could not replace the other.

By short walks through weary hours of struggle they reached the end of the glacier where they found a little spot of dry ground for a fire. Muir asked Dr. Young to rest there until he could hurry to the ship, miles away, for help. But Dr. Young pleaded with him not to leave him but to help him struggle on to the vessel. Long after sunrise they reached the ship-side and Muir called for help. Instead of hastening to them, the missionaries, irritated by the delay, began to reproach Dr. Young for going on a wild-goose chase. But the Captain, seeing the injured man, pushed them aside, exclaiming: "Oh,____, ____, this is no time for preaching. Don't you see the man is hurt?" Dr. Young was quickly taken aboard, and strong, skilled men put the other arm in its proper place. Then after a generous meal, he was put to bed and he slept all the way back to Wrangell.

Muir, in accustomed modesty, never mentioned or recorded this amazing rescue until a sensational caricature of the incident appeared in a magazine. Then Muir published the story in modest unheroic terms. However, Dr. Young in his book, Alaska Days with John Muir, described the fearful accident and Muir's marvelous work in carrying an injured and helpless man down a mountain wall. He gave full credit to him.

On one of the excursions in the boats with Dr. Young and Chief Kadachan, Muir and party visited a dead village which had been abandoned many years previous. There were many deserted dwellings largely in ruin but they showed astonishing workmanship. One dwelling was forty feet square built of planks two feet wide and six inches thick. The ridge pole was two feet in diameter and forty feet long. Nearby was a long line of carved totem poles. The missionary archaeologist called the deck hands to cut down one pole, saw out a figure, and carry it aboard ship. Chief Kadachan said to him: "How would you like to have an Indian go to your graveyard, break down and carry away a monument belonging to your family?" The matter was hushed up by apologies and gifts.

On a journey into the gold fields Muir met an old French Canadian miner named Le Claire. He lived by his mine in a log hut ten feet long and eight feet wide. He invited Muir to spend the night with him. The bed was too narrow for two people, so they spread their blankets on the floor, their heads under the bed, and their feet against the opposite wall. Le Claire was a well educated man, of pleasant speech, and his memory was stored with numerous tales of adventure and descriptions of birds, animals, and flowers. He loved all nature. All wild creatures trusted him and would eat out of his hand, and would come promptly at his call. Le Claire said he had a family of nine children, the youngest eight years old and his home was in Victoria. Muir loved meeting such interesting characters.

In the latter part of August Muir made a trip up the Stickeen River to explore the Dirt and Stickeen Glaciers. His base of travel was Buck's Station, a few miles below the Stickeen Glacier, which was kept by a friendly Frenchman named Choquette. Muir roamed over the great glaciers for days, carrying only a little package of food, a blanket and a tent-sheet. During the excursion it rained almost continually, but this did not hinder or disturb him. He worked his way along the Dirt Glacier for sixteen miles between "Yosemite" walls two to three thousand feet high. He found spots of moraine debris stranded on the ice where flowers were vigorously growing. In making his way aroud one sheer wall he had to fight his way, inch by inch, through a thorny thicket of Devil's Clubs. It was a painful experience.

Completing his study of the Dirt Glacier, Muir went to

the larger Stickeen. On it he found vast fields of ice and moraine material over which he scrambled with difficulty but with interest and pleasure. One evening he made his camp by a little lake, then wandered away for further exploration. It was raining steadily as later he tried to find his way back. He had to crawl through dense thickets on hands and knees, his clothes as wet as though he was swimming. He lost his way and had to climb a small tree for observation. Obtaining his bearings he soon got back to camp where he made a fire and a cup of tea. Then shedding his dripping-wet clothes, and wrapping himself in his blanket, he crept under the tent-sheet in pouring rain, "glad, rich, and almost comfortable."

In the morning he donned his soggy clothes, glad that they were "fresh and clean." (He always had something for which to be glad.) As a reward for his perseverance he soon discovered the rare plant, little "Calypso Borealis" and also one of his favorite creatures—the Douglas squirrel. These were compensations enough for him. Another night he had to spend by a glowing fire, "steaming and drying after being wet for two days and a night." Yet he remarked, "one might spend a whole joyful life" on such expeditions.

Then he went back to Wrangell to prepare for another long excursion. This one was to be a canoe voyage of eight hundred miles through straits, sounds, inlets and bays, among picturesque islands and on the rough open sea. Muir soon started this excursion taking along Indian Chiefs Toyatte and Kadachan and Indian interpreters and camp-makers, John and Charley. Also Dr. S. Hall Young joined him on the tour, hoping to prepare the way for Christian

114

missions among the Indian tribes. It was now late October with weather a mixture of sunshine, rain and snow. Once they were entertained by a Kake Indian family of distinction, father and mother, son and daughter, who said to them: "We always do to Boston (English) men as we have done to you, give a little of what we have, treat everybody well, and never quarrel." That night around the campfire they discussed their religion, ideas of the next world, the stars, the flowers, ways of animals, and many other things. Chief Kadachan interposed a surprising question to Dr. Young. "Have wolves souls?" The Indians thought they had.

At each village Dr. Young held services, singing hymns, praying and preaching. Everywhere the tribes welcomed the promise of school teachers and ministers to be sent among them. They said they enjoyed peace and plenty, but lacked a church and a school for their children. Frequently after Dr. Young's sermon, the Indians asked the "other Chief" (meaning Muir) to speak to them also. Muir tried to avoid a speech but they persisted in their request, so he talked to them about the wonders and beauties of God's creation, saying that God was the Father of all men everywhere, loving and planning good for all. Once after a service Dr. Young asked the interpreter, John, to report what the people had to say about the speeches. John said they were talking of Muir's address. "They say he knows how to talk, and beats the preacher far." Toyatte and Kadachan teased Dr. Young about this response.

During all of these October and November days, the party paddled their canoe into scores of mainland bays to observe the magnificent glaciers. They landed on gravelly

115

beaches where Dr. Young and Muir examined the great ice fields, their lateral and terminal moraines, and studied the beginnings on the distant snowy peaks. In Glacier Bay the water was dotted with massive icebergs, and at times new ones would split off the front wall of a glacier and plunge thunderously into the sea. The Indian crew was fearful of approaching the shore in the midst of such real dangers.

Among the most interesting and influential of the Indian tribes were the Chilcats. One chief's house was forty feet square, well built and clean. Its doors were neatly paneled, nibbled into shape by a small Indian adze. The Chief entertained the party at a well prepared dinner of baked potato, broiled salmon and fish-oil, and delicious wild berries. The Chief's steward closed the dinner with a loud announcement, saying in their language, "That's all." At the close of the evening service a very venerable old man arose to speak. He said, though an aged man, he was glad to listen to these new things the missionaries had to tell. He had often observed other white men who always seemed to be seeking only their own good, buying furs at smallest price possible. These traders and gold miners were like people living on the other side of a fast flowing and noisy stream. "Now," he said, "we whites and Indians are on the same side of the stream, eye to eye and heart to heart, and we are glad to keep silent and listen."

One morning on the voyage as the party was preparing to set out, they beheld one of the most beautiful sights ever seen. A distant peak turned red and the vivid color spread slowly over the vast landscape of other peaks, snow-fields, canyons and green forests, like a flood of flaming fire.

The party stood hushed and awe-struck as if they had seen the heavens opened and God himself appear. Muir said he did not know how long they watched. The landscape passed slowly through many bright, glowing colors to at last pale yellow and white. They rowed away with Muir feeling that Gloria in Excelsis was resounding in the heavens.

Leaving their last camp on November 21st, they returned to Ft. Wrangell in calm, bright weather and were met by friendly, cheering crowds. Muir learned that his steamer had left Wrangell eight days previous and he would be compelled to wait a month for the next one. His explorations were now closed by the approach of winter. Near the end of the year, 1879, Muir got a ship for Portland, Oregon. There on urgent requests he gave several lectures, and slipped away for a brief trip up the Columbia River. Early in the new year, 1880, he was home again in San Francisco. An immense accummulation of mail awaited him. Also, more important to him, a young lady in Alhambra Valley, was anxiously waiting too.

CHAPTER TEN

RANCHING, WRITING, CRUISING

Among the accumulated letters awaiting Muir's return from Alaska in January, 1880, was one from Mrs. Katharine Merrill Graydon. She was one of the three little children who visited and read to Muir in Indianapolis when he was confined to a dark room by an eye injury. Now grown up, married, and become a teacher, she had an occasion to write to him. In a class room two years previous Dr. David Starr Jordan had read an interesting article in Scribner's Magazine written by John Muir. It was the story of the water ouzel. Katharine proudly announced to Dr. Jordan and the class that she knew the author. She said in her letter: "The way my acquaintance of long ago developed into friendship, and the way I proudly said I knew you, would have made you laugh." The purpose of this letter, she said, was to introduce Dr. Jordan who was going soon to the Pacific Coast. To Muir this was a pleasing, heart-warming remembrance.

Early in the year John Muir and Louie Wanda Strentzel announced their wedding to take place on April 14th at the Strentzel home with Dr. I. E. Dwinell reading the ceremony. The Strentzel home was in Alhambra Valley which was originally known as "Canada Del Hambre" (Valley of Hunger). Mrs. Strentzel disliked this name and changed it to Moore's famous Spanish "Alhambra." Letters poured in upon the happy couple from friends who were completely taken by surprise. Mrs. John Swett's letter was typical of the reaction. She said the date "April" aroused laughing incredulity. But she added, "John (Dr. Swett) and I are jubilant over the match."

The wedding was simple and informal in the spirit and desire of the young couple, especially of the shy and bashful groom. And the day joined in the naturalist's honor with a furious rainstorm. Dr. and Mrs. Strentzel vacated the house in Alhambra Valley, turning it over to the Muirs, and moved to the frame house on the hill nearer Martinez. John Muir at once rented many acres of the Strentzel ranch and set about planting more orchards and vineyards. He had a natural aptitude and youthful training for horticultural work and enjoyed the occupation.

But soon the wilderness again was calling, and he had an unfinished explorative task in Alaska. Throughout their lives together, John and Wanda had a sympathetic understanding in regard to his nature excursions. Thus she graciously acquiesced when Thomas Magee proposed another summer tour to Alaska. They sailed from San Francisco on July 30th, again aboard the steamer California. John wrote daily letters to his young wife describing the voyage, the ports of Victoria, Nanaimo, Ft. Wrangell, and incidents on shipboard and on the excursions. Dr. S. Hall Young, his missionary friend, was waiting at the Wrangell dock where Muir's first words were: "When can you be ready to travel?"

After some minor excursions Dr. Young and Muir planned their major trip of exploration to Glacier Bay. Dr. Young had a little dog which he had named Stickeen. The little creature possessed most unusual intelligence and character. He became fondly attached to Muir, would follow him everywhere, lie at his feet, and sleep at his door. He seemed to understand everything said to him and would obey all orders. Stickeen went along with the party on the excursions.

They started north to Taylor and Glacier Bays on August 16th, taking in their large canoe three Indian servants, Stickeen, and all their supplies and equipment. They had delightful night camps along shore where the waters swarmed with salmon and snowy white mountain goats roamed on the slopes. Cascades lulled them to sleep. Fiords opened into the mountains with high Yosemite-like walls, bearing cliff gardens of ferns and flowers. Holkam Bay, locally known as Sumdum Bay, had two forks fifteen to twenty miles long, where the Bay waters reached to the foot of the side walls, affording few camping spots. After exploring up one of the forks six miles, they had to return to the Bay to find a bit of level shore. By the end of August they had arrived in Taylor Bay and pitched camp in front of a great glacier with a front wall seven miles wide.

On the next morning a wild storm was raging. Muir was curious to see what the appearance of the glacier would be in such weather. Without waiting for breakfast he put a few pieces of dry bread in his pocket and started on the trip. Stickeen immediately followed. And though Muir ordered him back, each time he would slip around and rejoin him. So Muir gave him a piece of his bread, and they trotted off together.

They walked along the forested edge of the glacier for about four miles, then Muir cut steps in the ice wall and man and dog climbed to the top. Here the storm, though abating some, yet carried such mist that it was difficult

121

to see to any distance. They wandered for miles over the icy surface, broken in places by narrow crevasses over which they could easily jump. Toward noon Muir could see the further side of the glacier where he found a little lake. At first he took it to be an arm of the Bay. But the water was fresh and his aneroid showed that it was a hundred feet above sea level. As evening approached, Muir and the dog started back across the seven miles of the glacier top, jumping a number of crevasses seven to eight feet wide. Then as darkness came on, they reached a crevasse forty feet wide. They walked miles up and down the crack but could discover no place narrow enough to jump.

However they did find a slim ice-bridge, perhaps five or more inches thick at the top which stretched across the chasm eight feet below the rim. As Muir gazed at this desperate way of getting across, Stickeen stood by him and whined pitifully. Muir decided that they could not spend the night there, nor retreat, so he began to cut footholds down the ice wall to the narrow bridge, while Stickeen ran along the crevasse looking for a better way across and crying bitterly. Muir, getting down to the bridge sliver, began cutting off its sharp edge to a four inch walk-way. The distance at this point was about seventy-five feet and the work was dangerous and toilsome. But at length he reached the other side, cut notches in the ice wall and gained the top in safety. Stickeen was now crying violently, and though Muir tried to reassure him, he only wailed the louder.

Muir walked a short distance away as though he intended to leave him, but Stickeen would not venture to cross. So

Muir talked to him in calm, soothing tones, insisting that he could follow if he would, otherwise he would perish. Gradually the little dog hushed his cries, slid his feet down the icy steps to the bridge, and walked cautiously across to the other wall. There he hesitated, while Muir encouraged him and leaned over to catch him if he made the attempt to climb the slippery steps to the top. With a sudden spring Stickeen leaped up the notches to safety. Then, wild with joy, he ran, barked, circled around, leaped past Muir who tried to stop him, and for some time continued his hysterical romping.

Finally, as darkness deepened, Muir calmed him down and they hastened off the glacier and down the side wall back to camp. They heard the Indians firing guns to guide them home. They were too tired for much of a dinner, and both man and dog were so nervously wrought up that neither could sleep long without dreaming of that narrow bridge and awakening with fright.

In Glacier Bay the party discovered another huge ice-field which they named the Muir Glacier. At a later date Muir was crossing its surface and in order to shorten his walk to camp, attempted to glissade down a snowy ravine, but struck a strip of ice which shot him into a pile of rocks. He suffered no particular harm, but two ravens had observed him and lit on a rock nearby with diabolical screams. Apparently they expected to feast on his dead body. Muir just brushed himself off and laughed at them saying: "Not yet. Not yet."

By autumn time Muir was back in Alhambra Valley, taking care of his fruit and glad to be home again with Wanda. During the winter days he made many improvements in the house, and occupied the stormy days with writing. In the spring of 1881 two matters of importance occurred. One was the birth of a baby daughter, Anna Wanda, on March 27th. Muir, fond of children, was thrilled with this event. The other matter was an invitation to join an expedition into Arctic waters in command of a friend, Capt. C. L. Hooper. The United States Government was sending him to discover the fate of the steamer Jeannette which had disappeared among the ice-floes in the Arctic circle. Its commander Capt. George W. DeLong was searching for a water way to the North Pole.

The family council approved Muir's acceptance of this opportunity to explore the north Alaska and Siberian lands, so he sailed from San Francisco on the U S. Revenue cutter Corwin on May 4th. The expedition continued its search for the Jeannette during all of the summer and until late October without finding any trace of the lost ship. Wherever the Corwin halted in ports or near strange islands of the Arctic Ocean, Muir was put ashore to make botanical and geological observations. His interesting accounts of these explorations appeared in the San Francisco Evening Bulletin and were later published in a book under the title, The Cruise of the Corwin.

While the Corwin was searching for the polar expedition the Jeannette had been crushed in the ice-floes and sunk about one hundred and fifty miles north of the New Siberian Islands on June 12th. Captain DeLong and his crew of thirty-four made their way in the ship's boats southward to the Siberian mainland, but only thirteen reached civilization in safety. DeLong and ten of his men died of starvation. Others were lost, but the Chief Engineer

Melville succeeded in reaching a Russian village and or-
ganized a rescue party in the following spring to bring
back the ship's records and the bodies of the crew.

During all of these months Muir faithfully wrote letters
to his wife but found infrequent chances to mail them.
And few letters from home could reach him. He wrote:
"My heart aches, not to go home ere I have done my work,
but just to know that you are well." Once he reported
the discovery of a dead Eskimo village on the St. Lawrence
Island in the Bering Sea. The people had died of starvation
and hunderds of skeletons were scattered around their
huts. The Corwin Smithsonian explorer collected a hundred skulls and piled them in a heap on board the ship.
Other men gathered guns, axes, spears, etc. and Muir
said he found a little box of a child's playthings which
might please Anna Wanda, but sagely added, "which I
suppose you will not let into the house."

Muir returned in the fall of the year to his home and
spent most of the next ten years, 1881-1891, in cultivating
and extending his Alhambra ranch, increasing its produc-
tion until, as he said, "I had more money than I thought I
would ever need for my family or for all expense of travel
and study." The ranch required his personal supervision
during the harvest months and spring pruning, but his
summers were usually free for his nature excursions. In addition to his ranch income he was paid $100.00 to $250.00
for magazine articles. The family was now in very comfortable circumstances.

Wanda Muir was not a good traveler but visited the
Yosemite with John in the summer of 1884. Writing home
to her parents and little daughter she revealed her error in

mistaking "trout for catfish," and feared "a bear behind every bush." But she felt that John's health was becoming impaired by incessant toil on the ranch and insisted that they stay in the mountains until he was well and strong again. She also thought that John was neglecting his nature studies and writing which were more important than ranching. She was loyal to John's major interests in life.

In the summer of 1885 Muir had one of his strange premonitions. One day he suddenly recalled that he had not seen his parents or any of the family for eighteen years and the impression filled his mind that unless he went back to the old home now, he would never again see his father alive. His father had fallen some years before and broken a hip, which left him a cripple. He was now living in Kansas City with a daughter, while John's mother was still in the old Wisconsin home. John went first to Wisconsin and asked his brother David and his mother to go with him to see the father, saying that unless they went now they would never again see him alive. They were greatly surprised since there had been no change in the father's condition. John also wrote to the other sisters to join him at Kansas City. He visited his brother Daniel in Lincoln, Nebraska, with a similar request. All gathered about the father's bedside for a few days, then one night he peacefully passed away.

In a reminiscent letter to his wife, John wrote that few lives had been more restless, toilsome, clean and devoted, though with strange delusions, than that of his father. Toward the close of his life he had often spoken of his cruel mistakes with his children, especially with his "dear wandering son, John." After the funeral Muir returned to the

126

scenes of his youth on the Wisconsin farm and visited with his friends of those other days.

In 1886 another daughter, Helen, was born to the Muirs, filling their home with new charm and pleasure. But it was a common concern of many of Muir's friends that he was neglecting his literary work. Thus he was influenced to accept the proposal of the J. Dewing Company to edit an illustrated publication entitled, Picturesque California. This required many new excursions over the West. With his artist friend, William Keith, he visited the Puget Sound country. They traveled as far north as Vancouver and Victoria. One excursion took them to Mt. Hood and Mt. Rainier. Muir wrote regarding Mt. Rainier: "I did not mean to climb it, but got excited and was soon on the top." He was not feeling well at the time, but mountain climbing was never a problem to him. In order to avoid the interruptions by ranch work, he did his writing in a hotel room in San Francisco. But this was dreary, confining work, and he was glad when it was done.

In 1889 John Muir was called into a new and important assignment. Cattle, sheep, and lumber men had been making havoc of the upper Yosemite region, under the slack and often mismanagement of the State authorities. A movement was now started to change the Yosemite State Park into a National Park and add a vast area along the crest of the Sierra bordering it on the east. Robert Underwood Johnson, Editor of the Century Magazine, proposed that Muir take him and a group of prominent Californians, including the Governor, into the Yosemite on a camping trip in June, 1889, and that Muir write a series of articles on the Yosemite for his magazine. This Muir did, arousing a remarkable response from the general public across the nation. But there was a fierce, uphill fight in both Congress and in the California Legislature where lumber and grazing men put up bitter opposition. But Congress approved the project in 1890, providing the State would release its control. California did not accede to this proposal for several years.

In October, 1890, Dr. John Strentzel died leaving his widow alone in the big house on the hill. Mrs. Strentzel invited the Muirs to live with her and they accepted, leaving the Alhambra house after ten years of residence there. The new home, though larger, was less cozy and homey. Muir now turned the management of the ranch over to a foreman, so that he could be free to follow his scientific pursuits and literary work. In the foregoing winter he had suffered a severe attack of the grippe which left an annoying bronchial cough. As a cure, he spent the months of July and August in another Alaska trip to Glacier Bay.

CHAPTER ELEVEN

FAR HORIZONS OF EARTH

In the spring of 1891 in response to a request of Robert Underwood Johnson, Muir drew a map showing the boundary lines of a new Sequoia National Park, for a bill introduced in Congress that year. This act finally became a law about thirty years later. For years Muir had been strenuously advocating the protection and preservation of our national forests. The first of such bills was passed by Congress on March 3rd, 1891, and was signed into law by President Harrison. But tremendous fighting was yet to be required to conserve the forests and playgrounds for future generations. Muir led in the formation of the Sierra Club on June 4th, 1892, which had both of these aims in view. He was president of this club for the rest of his life.

The famous Hoosier poet, James Whitcomb Riley, lectured in San Francisco about this time, and Muir, modestly as usual, introduced himself as simply John Muir. Mr. Riley apparently could not think who he was. Dr. David Starr Jordan happened to be standing near and remarked: "Mr. Riley, this man is the author of the Muir Glacier." This brought a quick recognition.

In 1893 Muir decided to fulfill his long-dreamed-of plan of travel to the distant lands of all the Earth. In the spring of the year he visited his old Wisconsin home, then went on to Chicago for the World's Fair. He thought it was like a pack-rat's nest, holding many things both of rubbish and great value. The architecture of the buildings, landscap-

ing, art gallery paintings, were beautiful. But he soon hastened on to New York where he finished some articles for
the Century Magazine. The Associate Editor, Robert Underwood Johnson, introduced him to John Burroughs, the
naturalist; Richard Watson Gilder, editor-in-chief; Gifford
Pinchot, and other prominent New Yorkers. Everywhere
Muir's audiences insisted on hearing the story of the little
dog, Stickeen. Porters, waiters, clerks, strangers, slipped
into the banquet room, hid behind doors, curtains, or under tables, in order to listen. Robert Underwood Johnson
escorted Muir to famous homes and places in New England
and the East: to the home of Henry Fairfield Osborn
on the Hudson; to Boston, Concord, Walden Pond; the
graves of Emerson and Thoreau in Sleepy Hollow Cemetery, and numerous historic monuments and buildings. In
Concord they dined with the son of Emerson. On the
porch they met the father-in-law, Judge Keyes, who as
Mr. Johnson introduced himself, remained seated in apparent unconcern. But as Muir's name was spoken, he excitedly sprang to his feet, exclaiming: "John Muir, is this
John Muir?" and enthusiastically shook his hand.

Back in Boston they were entertained at the home of
Prof. Charles Sprague Sargent, director of the Arnold
Arboretum, whose place and grounds, Muir said, were the
finest mansion and grounds he had ever seen. He met many
famous editors and writers, and at Harvard University
was introduced to Professors Royce, Porter, and Park-
man.

Then Muir sailed from New York to Liverpool and went
on to Edinburgh. Dr. Johnson had given him a letter of introduction to the famous publisher, David Douglas. The

publisher was dignified and indifferent until he suddenly recalled who Muir was, then he "burst forth into the warm-est cordiality and became a gushing fountain of fun, hu-mor, and stories of old Scotch writers." Dr. Douglas took him to all the famous places of the city, then to dinner at his home, telling anecdotes of John Brown, Walter Scott, Hugh Miller, etc. Muir said it was "the most wonderful night as far as humanity is concerned, I ever had in the World."

Then he hastened on to Dunbar, which as a boy he had left forty-four years before. Here he was amid the scenes of his youth and with relatives and friends, strangely grown old. He went again to his old home, the school, Dunbar Castle ruins, scenes of so many escapades, joyous and pain-ful. The teacher at the school had been there all but two years of Muir's absence. Someone said to him: "Mr. Dick, don't you wish you had the immortal glory of having whipped John Muir?" Ten days Muir roamed about the old town of so many memories, then went on to Glasgow, Stirling, Inversnaid, Loch Katrine, and Loch Lomond. Heather was in bloom and he loathed to tear himself away. By September 1st he was in London, visiting Kew Gardens and its distinguished botanist, Sir Joseph Hooker. Later he visited Killarney in Ireland "to see the beautiful bogs and lakes." And on September 16th, sailed from Liverpool for New York and home.

Muir turned again to his writing and in the autumn of 1894 his first major book, The Mountains of California, was published by the Century Press. It was hailed with delight and the first edition was quickly exhausted. Muir now planned to complete his book on The Yosemite and spent six weeks of the summer of 1895 in revisiting those familiar scenes. The Yosemite Park was still under State control. The Valley floor was fenced in with barbed wire and three hundred horses were pastured in it each night. Tourist travel had largely decreased.

In June of 1896 Harvard University honored Muir with a Master of Arts degree. And in 1911 Yale University gave him another honorary degree. In playful mood he described this occasion: "We donned our academic robes . . . shining like crow blackbirds . . . when my name was called I arose with a grand air, shook my massive academic plumes into finest fluting folds . . . stepped forward in awful majesty and stood rigid and solemn like an ancient sequoia while the orator poured praise on the honored wanderer's head . . ." Muir was not greatly impressed with academic honors.

In the spring of 1896, Muir had another of his strange premonitions, this time regarding his mother's death. He felt that he must go at once to visit her in Wisconsin, and summoned his brothers and sisters to meet him there. They objected, saying that she was as well as usual, but when John arrived at the old home, two of the daughters met him at the door saying, "John, God must have sent you, for mother is very sick." She died in about a week.

While on this trip, John went on to New York, visiting John Burroughs and Henry Fairfield Osborn, then back to Milwaukee where he found William Trout, his friend of the Canada tour. Another pleasant visit was with his friends of the Indianapolis days there.

At this time the U. S. Forestry Commission, under chairman Charles Sprague Sargent, invited Muir to join in the survey of the country's forests. The other members of the

Commission were: Professors Brewer and Hague, and Alexander Agassiz, Gifford Pinchot, and General Abbot. The Commission explored the forests of the country and its report to Congress helped to establish many forest reserves. The University of Wisconsin later gave Muir an LL.D. honorary degree in recognition of his service in this work.

Following this tour by the Commission, Muir joined Prof. Sargent and William M. Canby in a study of the forests of the Rocky Mountains, in the United States, Canada and into Alaska. Muir wrote a series of articles on this study which appeared in the Harper's Weekly and the Atlantic Monthly. Walter Hines Page, Editor of the Atlantic Monthly, was greatly impressed with Muir's writings, and visited him in Alhambra Valley. Page published the Atlantic articles in book form under the title, Our National Parks.

In the autumn of 1898, Muir, Sargent and Canby were off on another tour, roaming through the forests of the Allegheny Mountains, going southward through the Carolinas, Tennessee, Georgia, and Alabama. They crossed many of the trails Muir had made in his Thousand Mile Walk to the Gulf. Later with Sargent he crossed Florida along his old trail to Cedar Keyes. There he found Mrs. Hodgson who had nursed him back to health many years before. When he announced his name, she shouted, "John Muir? My California John Muir?" There were many such pleasant reunions on this trip.

In the summer of 1899 Mr. E. H. Harriman invited John Muir to go with him on the Harriman Alaska Expedition on his ship the Elder, under command of Capt. F. A. Doran.

With him were John Burroughs, Prof. Brewer, and other naturalists. Muir reported later that this was one of the most delightful trips of his life. The ship was very comfortable, the group discussions interesting, and Mr. Harriman a gracious host. Muir spoke of the ship as a hotel, a club, a home, and a floating university. Out of the fellowship came a visit to Harriman's Pelican Lodge on Klamath Lake where Mr. Harriman pursuaded Muir to dictate the story of My Boyhood and Youth to Harriman's private secretary.

During the next three years Muir made many return visits to his beloved Yosemite and the Range of Light, writing many articles in favor of forest reserves and national parks. In 1903 he went on a world tour with Prof. Sargent and his son, Robeson, visiting the parks, gardens, art galleries, in Berlin, St. Petersburg, Moscow. Then they crossed Siberia and Manchuria to Japan and Shanghai. There the Sargents and Muir went separate ways, Muir going alone to India, Egypt, Ceylon, Australia, New Zealand, Malay Peninsula, Manila and Hong Kong. There he took a ship for Honolulu and home.

Just prior to this world tour, President Theodore Roosevelt visited California, May 15, 1903, and asked Muir to go camping with him in the upper regions of the Yosemite Park. He wanted to see what should be done in respect to a national park and forest reserves. Roosevelt and Muir slipped away from the crowd and spent three wonderful days together in a high Sierra camp. They were ever afterward lifelong and intimate friends. Roosevelt was convinced of the correctness of Muir's views on parks and reserves, and acted promptly in establishing them. Yosemite became a National Park in 1905.

Misfortune and sorrow befell Muir in August, 1905. His daughter Helen had been ill and was convalescent at Daggett, on the Mohave Desert. Muir was visiting her there, when a telegram reached him telling him of his wife's serious illness. He hurried home where Louie Wanda died a few days later. Thereafter the house on the hill was only a shelter, never again a home. While on the desert with Helen, Muir discovered a wonderful petrified forest which his friend, President Roosevelt, established as a National Monument in 1906.

The death of his wife brought an epoch of Muir's life to a sad close. In the following four years he wrote but little and traveled scarcely at all. He remarked in 1911: "During these few later years of domestic troubles and anxieties but little writing or studying of any sort has been possible. But these fortunately are now beginning to abate and I hope that something worth while may still be accomplished."

Thus a long deferred excursion to South America was undertaken. In the middle of August, 1911, he sailed from New York for Para, Brazil. There he took the river steamer, Dennis, up the Amazon, and spent a week at Manaos, exploring the noble forests with a Yale graduate, a Mr. Sanford, stationed there. Then he visited the beautiful city and bay of Rio de Janeiro and later shipped to Santos where he walked as he said, a thousand miles through the forests of the aboriginal Araucaria trees. His journeys also took him to Buenos Aires, and over the Andes Mountains to Santiago, Chile. After a five hundred mile trip down the coast line of Chile, he returned to the east coast at Monte-video, where he prepared to sail for Teneriffe in the Canary Islands. From Teneriffe he went to Cape Town, South Africa, and journeyed northward to the Zambesi baobab forests and the Victoria Falls. His jaunts took him to Beira on the east coast, then by boat to Mombasa, where he went inland to the Nyanza Lake region. Back at Mombasa he started homeward by way of the Suez Canal, Naples, to New York. It was a long satisfying tour. He now felt that he had seen all of the great mountain ranges of the world. He still insisted that the Sierras, his Range of Light, were the most beautiful mountains of them all.

In these few remaining years of his life Muir lived quiet-ly at home doing some writing, or occasionally making a visit to the home of some friend. He was always a welcome guest. And there were his daughters, Wanda on the ranch in Alhambra Valley, and Helen at Daggett on the desert. Wanda had three boys and Helen two. Muir once re-marked: "I'm in my old library den, the house desolate, nobody living in it save a hungry mouse or two . . . dearly cherished memories about it and the fine garden grounds full of trees, bushes, and flowers that my wife and father-in-law and I planted, fine things from every land."

In December of 1914 Muir left the Martinez home for a visit with Helen at Daggett. There he fell ill with pneumonia and was rushed to a hospital in Los Angeles, where he died on Christmas Eve, with sheets of his manu-script, Travels in Alaska, lying on the bed around him.

CHAPTER TWELVE

JOHN MUIR'S SERVICE TO THE WORLD

John Muir was a distinguished naturalist and almost equally at home in a number of fields of exploration. He was a botanist, a geologist, ornithologist, entomologist, and well informed in all related fields. He was a skilled mechanic, an inventive genius, master of farm labor and horticulture, an unsurpassed mountaineer, a world traveler, and exceptional as a lecturer and writer. Yet, with it all he was shy, humble, self-effacing. He was so forthright, enthusiastic, magnetic, that he drew the hearts of all honorable folk to him.

Muir was a nature-lover, and believed that all creatures were endowed with certain rights and powers by their Creator. They were not just the property of man to be used or abused at his whim. His long life of kindly approach to all living things, tame and wild, produced many striking examples of understanding and fellowship. There were good and bad among them as in the human species.

John Muir was a humanitarian, a defender of the rights and enjoyments of people everywhere. His great achievements lay in his leadership in the establishment of National Parks and Forest Reservations. His dependable and unmistakable knowledge in these fields of natural and human value, coupled with an amazing literary exposition of the situations, appealed to the country's leading magazines and newspapers and captured the spirit and heart of the nation and its leaders. He has been rightly called the Father of our National Parks and Forest Reservations. And the preservation of the forests prevented the denudation of fertile soils from vast areas of the country and the resulting silt in streams and lakes.

During the last twelve years of his life he fought to preserve the beautiful Hetch Hetchy Valley and the Grand Canyon of the Tuolumne as a vacation area of the Yosemite National Park. Politicians wanted the Hetch Hetchy Valley for a reservoir of water for the City of San Francisco. Geologists and surveyors pointed out that there were other locations where the water could be impounded, though at somewhat higher cost. Thus one of the beauty spots of the world, second only to the Yosemite Valley, was lost to the whole people just to save a few dollars. Muir had proposed a road be built along the Merced River into and across the upper regions of the Park to Tuolumne Meadows, thence down the Grand Canyon of the Tuolumne, through the Hetch Hetchy, and over the ridge to the Yosemite Valley. This would have opened a vast new area to vacationers. Dr. C. Hart Merriam said the Hetch Hetchy reservoir was a monumental mistake but Muir added that it was a monumental crime.

John Muir's service to the world was not simply in the things he discovered and publicized. He was himself one of the great contributions to humanity's treasure of mind and spirit. He had risen above poverty, hardships, restrictions, that would have broken the heart of most people to become a world-famous individual, modest, gentle, affable and gracious. In conversation he possessed a magnetism and attraction that few mortals have ever acquired. A convention in Yosemite Valley once offered him $100.00 just to be present at the meeting.

Muir's friendships were numerous, intimate and exceptional in depth and variety. Common folk and the great of the earth were happy to own a place in his charmed circle. Among them were many educators like John Swett, Ezra Carr, J. D. Butler; scientists like Charles S. Sargent, Asa Gray, Joseph Hooker; writers like Ralph Waldo Emerson, John Burroughs, Robert Underwood Johnson; businessmen like E. H. Harriman and John Bidwell; rulers like Theodore Roosevelt, and artists like William Keith. But a miner in his lonely hut, a bright-eyed boy in tattered clothes on a backwoods farm, a little dog at his heels, a squirrel, a bird of the forest, all had a welcome to his heart.

John Muir bequeathed to the world a number of beautiful books. These were most interesting when he kept close to his notes and letters in which he exhibited such remarkable sprightliness and spontaneity. Book writing was mechanical and tedious to him, but clothed in the glow of his field notations and intimate letters they hold the charm and magnetism of his unrivaled conversation. Much in his extensive notes and letters has never been published. But these published books represent his best writing: The Mountains of California; My First Summer in the Sierra; The Story of My Boyhood and Youth; A Thousand Mile Walk to the Gulf; Travels in Alaska; The Cruise of the Corwin; The Yosemite; Steep Trails; and two little books, Stickeen (his dog of Alaska trails) and Edward H. Harriman, a tribute.

John Muir was a scientific observer of unusual skill and success, not simply in one restricted field, but in many such as in geology, botany, ornithology, entomology and allied subjects. To him was given the credit of discovering living glaciers in the high Sierra, and their work in shaping and polishing the contours of peaks and canyons. The Yosemite Valley, the Muir Glacier, the National Parks, and our glorious forest reservations, stand as a memorial to him. But he was also an inventive genius. Who can say how far he might have gone in that direction had he given his life to such work? Many new plants and insects were first discovered by him, and added to the world's knowledge. He was a world traveler, and deserved the address he once gave himself, "John Muir, Earth Planet, Universe."

John Muir has been an inspiration to millions of people over the world, especially to youth. He had a brilliant mind, a marvelous memory, a winsome personality. The dreadful toil and drudgery of his youth left no bitterness in his soul. His father's religious fanaticisms never turned him away from his love of the New Testament. It was always his treasure. He was not a regular church-goer, but he gave more devout worship to God than probably most of the regular attendants. He was no iconoclast, no querulous objector to the religious observances of others, yet held some Biblical notions to which the dogmatists would object. John Muir was surely close to the spirit of the Great Teacher who said: "By this shall all men know that ye are my disciples, if ye have love one to another."

Finally, what do Contra Costa County and the city of Martinez owe to the memory of John Muir? Here he lived for thirty-four years, about one half of his life. Here he raised his family, and here he wrote many of his famous magazine articles and books, classics in the nature literature of the world. Here the great of the earth made a path to his door.

Communities, cities, nations, build monuments to their distinguished sons and preserve their dwelling places as objects of veneration. To many a lesser genius and public servant magnificent memorials have been erected in all lands. Others remember. SHALL WE FORGET?

The old John Muir house on the hill stands lonely, shabby, ghostly, among its unkempt remnants of his world-gathered ornamental trees and shrubs. His grave is in a little private cemetery at the end of a dusty orchard lane. The public, not the relatives, should be responsible for a stately, flower-lined avenue leading to his resting place with parking area for cars. The world will not forget John Muir. We may be judged for our neglect. Let us, his City, County, State, build a fitting memorial to his name.

The End.